SPEAK

AMERICAN

TOO

SPEAK AMERICAN TOO

YOUR GUIDE TO BUILDING POWERFUL BRANDS IN THE NEW HEARTLAND

PAUL JANKOWSKI

New Heartland Group Publishing Company
Brentwood, Tennessee

First published in 2014 by:
New Heartland Group Publishing Company
8115 Isabella Lane, Suite 11
Brentwood TN 37027

For ordering information or special discounts for bulk purchases, please contact info@newheartlandgroup.com.

Speak American® is a registered trademark of Access Brand Strategies.

Cover, interior and illustrations by Doug Cordes

Printed in the United States of America.

ISBN 978-0-9960917-0-1

First Edition

Dedication

This book is dedicated to fighters, warriors and never-give-uppers. As we'll discuss, the New Heartland is all about a set of core values. These values hold us together and are what we go to when we're happy and when things are tough.

My little sister, Teri Trotter, embodies these values like no one I know: a marathon-running, boot camp-instructing, real estate-selling, karaoke-singing, and general bad mamma-jamma. She crushed breast cancer after gut-wrenching rounds of chemo and radiation at the age of 38. A few months after celebrating her 5th anniversary of being cancer free, the stuff came back. Currently in the middle of her second round of chemo, she's fighting it again. And winning.

She started The Pink Wig Foundation to provide pink wigs for women who lost their hair due to their cancer treatments to give them hope and the "I will kick your butt, cancer" attitude. The Pink Wig Foundation also funds genetic testing and provides people going through cancer treatments with a more dignified/ private experience. See www.thepinkwig.com.

Thank you to all caregivers, doctors, nurses, scientists, and sponsors of research to end cancer and the many other insidious diseases we've all been affected by.

Thank You

This project would have never been completed without Carla Denham. Her superior ability to manage unwieldy projects such as this, see the broad vision, and have the patience to bring all the elements and people together for the common cause is remarkable. Most importantly, her passion for the content of this book and her commitment to core values and the effect they have on every part of life is greatly appreciated.

Ashley Darling played a key role in making this book happen. She's a terrific researcher/writer/do-all'er and I thank her for dealing with my constantly changing schedule and missing of deadlines. Her positive, easy-going attitude was always appreciated.

Kristy Lucero was a huge help with research and helping keep me on track. McKenzie Masters and Jen Mears were very valuable members of the team as well.

Special Thanks

Twenty-five years of dealing with my dream-chasing, entrepreneur-fueled craziness has earned my wife Sandra a special place in Heaven. A remarkable woman on all levels, she is the personification of the role a commitment to faith, community and family (among others) play in creating such a beautiful person inside and out.

CONTENTS

FOREWORD

Oftentimes, I find myself sitting in a meeting or on a conference call, fielding questions about the New Heartland. Many branding teams on the coasts put the area that largely consists of the southwestern, southeastern, and midwestern United States into the same bucket as the rest of the country.

Through my years working with brands in strategy, consumer engagement, promotions, and event/celebrity sponsorships, I've seen that the messaging many companies are putting out isn't resonating with this important group of consumers. I've lived and worked in the New Heartland my entire life, so I have the advantage of firsthand knowledge of how things work around here.

My agency specializes in building brands in the New Heartland. We love living and working here. And we are absolutely thrilled to help our clients thrive here, which is why we conducted an extensive study to supplement our third-party research.

Our research turned up some startling conclusions proving that the New Heartland has key differences from the rest of the country. These idiosyncrasies have a big impact on how brands connect with us. They also tell a lot about how core values and lifestyle affect our buying behavior.[1]

After analyzing the results and hearing the feedback from my clients, I knew we had to get this information out. The New Heartland represents almost 60 percent of the nation, so it's imperative that marketers everywhere take notice. My first book on the subject, *How to Speak American: Building Brands in the New Heartland*, was a broad cultural study, but I felt we could expand upon it. In this edition, you'll get it all—our research, case studies, and, most importantly, how to turn this information into an actionable plan for your brand.

So let's get to work. You might not know our language yet, but soon you'll Speak American™ too.

PAUL JANKOWSKI
President, New Heartland Group

INTRODUCTION

What are some of the stereotypes branding executives living outside the New Heartland associate with people living in the New Heartland? These are actual comments:

> *"(It's) not a stereotype ... they wear their ignorance and intolerance proudly."*

> *"Blue collar. Religious. Middle income. Drives a truck. Works at same job for years. Not in tune with latest technology."*

> *"Hillbillies, Bible-beaters, right-wing extremists."*

> *"Modernized rednecks."*

> *"Backwards, redneck, stuck in the past, close-minded."*

I know you're bombarded with things that occupy just about every minute of your day and only want to invest time in something that provides tangible value.

If you hang with me through this branding "field manual," I'm confident it will be worth your time investment. I guarantee you'll have a better understanding of how to build your brand in the New Heartland. Gaining even a tiny lift in brand equity with this powerful group of consumers is the difference between mediocrity and success.

This book gives you a glimpse into the lives of an enormous group of Americans, residing in a region that is home to *60 percent of this nation's loyal consumers and brand advocates.* Equally important, I'll show you specific ways to target the New Heartland consumer with practical examples of campaigns that worked and some that didn't. I'll also provide significant research that will undoubtedly challenge your existing knowledge and broaden your thinking about why you need to make the New Heartland a part of your brand plans.

This book is a follow-up to my 2011 book, *How to Speak American: Building Brands in the New Heartland,* which was part cultural immersion and part social observation. It set out to define the New Heartland consumer and trace the role core values play in buying behavior. Now that this group has been defined, let's get real on how to build a relationship with them and become experts in building campaigns that Speak American™.

Purposely provocative, Speak American™ is my way of challenging brands to be culturally relevant in their messaging. No, the New Heartland isn't more American than anywhere else in the country, but it does have its own language—a language that's built on distinct dialects, colloquialisms, inferred meanings, local definitions, and tradition-rich nuances all driven by long-standing cultural influences. We understand English but speak American. Brands wanting to reach us need to speak our language to be successful beyond a consumer transaction.

Odds are, you play some role in building brands that will benefit if the New Heartland consumer is won over. You might even share the views of the marketing executives that I quoted earlier. If either is true, allow me to help you take a more-informed approach to this massive segment of America.

We have a few key contrasts with the rest of the country. And we're okay with that. Actually, there's a lot of pride in our differences. This book is a tool you can use to get to know us better. If all goes well, you might even change your mind about some preconceived notions. There's also the chance that some of those notions will be reinforced. But if your brand is trying to reach us, you really need to study up on what makes us tick and, more importantly, why we engage with the brands we love. The fact that the New Heartland accounts for such a large group of potential customers is a great motivator. Plus, the affinity for core values-driven connections makes these consumers ideal brand advocates: if you can win them over, you are likely to keep them ... for generations. Not a bad payout for a relatively small investment in cultural education.

I've been waving the New Heartland banner for more than two decades. It's mind-boggling that from what I've seen, most marketers still don't understand the New Heartland. At all. Marketers waste time and resources rooted in business school-derived tactics and a short-sighted point of view. Regardless of the strength of the results, they are only a fraction of what they could have been. The New Heartland consumer is a unique segment that is ever-evolving and requires constant attention by brand managers for their brands to remain relevant. You don't launch a company website or Facebook page, then walk away. It needs constant attention, compelling content, and daily interaction with your audience. It's the same with building a New Heartland strategy.

I'm a New Heartland native ... born in Illinois and raised in Tennessee, and I'll serve as your guide as we make you a better New Heartland brand builder. We'll cover cultural nuances and purchase-driving passions, but we'll also discuss the top principles that form the foundation upon which everyday decisions are made. We're going to provide some great insight into how your brand can get invited to a family gathering (the ultimate inner circle). The findings presented here are a mix of research, case studies, and input from marketing industry experts. I also include my own personal experiences and insight as a professional of twenty-five-plus years in the branding world.

No marketer of any merit would assume their own life experiences were representative of such a large population, right? So, I hopped into my F-150 and took a drive—a really long drive. Actually, I took several really long drives around the New Heartland to meet the people who live, work, and play here.

Over the course of writing about the New Heartland, I've driven thousands of miles and had conversations with hundreds of New Heartland residents. I've done this to find out how they self-identify, what they find to be most important in their lives, and how they define their core values. You'll find snippets of these conversations scattered throughout this book and at www.newheartlandgroup.com.

After comparing what I had heard to a significant amount of primary and third-party research, I began to see the correlation between our values and brand loyalties, beliefs, and buying habits. Our life-styles have a lot to do with these core truths. Understanding them can provide an entry point for brands to start the conversation and ultimately build a trusted friendship.

But talking to New Heartlanders and using third-party research gave me only part of the story. I wanted to get some hard evidence that backed up the idea that we really are a unique group of consumers.

I commissioned a New Heartland Consumer Insights Study through an independent research firm, Nashville-based Prince Market Research, on what drives American consumers. We dove into their interests and values. We found where they spent their time and money. Then we separated the feedback into two groups—those who reside in the New Heartland and those who do not—to compare results.

Our findings confirmed our previous research. We're similar to the rest of the United States in many ways, but there are key differences that shape the very essence of our identities. These differences directly influence our buying decisions, brand loyalty, and attitudes toward brands. This extensive study really brought clarity to these facts.

Throughout the course of this book, I'll be sharing insights from this report and other research to serve as a foundation of the New Heartland consumer as a cultural segment versus a demographic. These findings are marketing gold. The report covers everything from music preferences and weekend hobbies to brands we support and our opinions on the current state of advertising. In simple numbers, you'll see just how important our values should be to your brand.

Please hear me when I say that the values I will discuss are not exclusive to the New Heartland. There are pockets of communities and individuals all over the country that share similar beliefs. In fact, you will probably find you have a lot in common with us. I only mean to present what drives *us* in *our* everyday decisions, big and small. These values are inextricably woven into all aspects of our lives, and by understanding them, present the greatest opportunity for brands to create lasting relationships with New Heartland consumers. New Heartland values tend to be more at the surface and part of everyday conversations. It's not unusual, for example, to learn where a new acquaintance goes to church, where their kids go to school, and who among your extended families know each other, in the first couple of conversations with a New Heartlander.

This book offers an unapologetic look at what it means to be from the New Heartland and why brands should care. Don't expect political correctness. You get enough of that from the media. Instead, I'm going to tell it like it is, New Heartland style.

I realize there are a few of you out there who actually do understand us. If you are among the minority, hopefully you saved your receipt.

For the others, let's get after it...

NEW HEARTLAND

▼

CULTURAL
SEGMENT

This cultural segment is underserved and largely dismissed, which presents a huge opportunity for brands who become New Heartland-savvy. It is my mission to make sure that by the time you finish reading this book, your brand will be among them.

One of the key takeaways is understanding and accepting the fact that the New Heartland is driven by cultural attitudes, traditions, and idiosyncrasies.

Carlos Saavedra, director of culture marketing at PepsiCo Beverages America, understands the difference between cultural and demographic marketing. "Like many companies, our traditional approach to multicultural marketing involved narrowing in on specific ethnic groups and developing campaigns specifically targeted to them. Now we are taking a much more expansive view of culture to provide content that is relevant to our consumer, regardless of ethnicity. It is no longer about marketing to a specific ethnic group, but about finding shared interests across different facets of culture that align with our brands," Saavedra said.

He goes on to say: "No longer do multicultural consumers feel like they are only part of one culture; rather, they feel comfortable picking and choosing parts of different cultures—for example, skate culture, sneaker culture, or foodie culture. It is more cost-effective for our brands to create content around a shared interest rather than creating separate content for individual demographic groups."

The New Heartland is not a demographic group; it consists of multiple ethnicities. It's home to a massive Latino and African-American/Black population. Ethnicity is very important to consumers, but it's not the only way they view themselves. Being aware of the cross-cultural impact on consumers is critical. This is where *core values come into play as the common thread* that weaves through all New Heartland cultures and ethnicities. Values are an equalizer in a cultural landscape riddled with challenges of reaching multi-dimensional groups with relevant and scalable messaging.

In recent years, brands and marketers have started to discover that one size does not fit all in this melting pot of a country. New strategies and even new agencies have been created by those who realized the need for more effective messages that speak to specific groups of people. At the same time, that messaging needs to be interesting to those cross-cultural consumers.

The Latino population, which has increased by more than 15 million in the last ten years, has created a marketing industry of its own. Many agencies have dedicated teams working to reach this very important group, with great success. Their buying power of an esti-mated 1.2 trillion dollars[2] is enough to get industries across the board interested in this growing group.

An ad campaign that appeals to groups in New England might not resonate with the same segment on the Plains. Brands are spending large amounts of money on messaging that falls on deaf ears.

Brands don't need to change the message to fit the New Heartland, just the way it's delivered.

We'll later discuss a great example of how Mountain Dew accomplished this.

Too many brands and their agencies along the East and West Coasts assume that all Americans fit neatly into little categories: Moms in San Francisco and San Antonio are driven by the same values. All twentysomethings, regardless of where they live, follow the same fashion trends. Doctors in the suburbs of Boston have similar lifestyles as doctors in Peoria, Lubbock, and Macon. But you know what they say about assuming.

All the research in the world is useless if you get some of the basic information wrong. Research is only as good as the questions you ask, the people who answer them, and how that information is put into action.

Do you know how to pronounce Mount Juliet or Lebanon in the local Tennessean dialect? Every few weeks, I hear a different radio spot where one of those communities is mispronounced. The words are said properly, but the local Southern spin on the name of the community isn't accounted for. How do you think consumers feel about brands that don't take the time to learn how to correctly pronounce their own town's name? Ouch. It's kinda like giving a diabetic dinner guest a huge piece of cake for dessert. Brands have to know who they're serving.

Now let's talk about who's invited to the table.

Probably the most-taught rule in marketing is Pareto's Principle: 80 percent of effects come from 20 percent of the causes. Or, as far as brands are concerned, 80 percent of sales come from 20 percent of customers. Marketers take this to heart and thus play to the base. The strategy is to find the core customers and retain their loyalty while increasing the frequency of their purchases. There is evidence to suggest that this might not be the most effective strategy in all cases.

Byron Sharp, author of *How Brands Grow: What Marketers Don't Know*, challenges the rules of marketing as we know it, and he's gotten the attention of some big names. Global brands such as Mars are now using Sharp's book to help direct their own strategies. Among the mountains of data presented, he makes a compelling case against relying completely on the 80/20 principle.

Here are some interesting points Sharp made on this subject:

- Some terminology that offers a misleading interpretation of your base customer is the "frequent buyer" category. Depending on the nature of the product, oftentimes, a frequent buyer is one who purchases a brand's goods only a few times a year. This is because of the averages between those who buy daily and those who rarely buy. Thus, very light buyers are put into a frequent-buyer category.

- Ignoring potential future sales can be of great detriment. Since the frequent-buyer category becomes open to those of occasional purchases, brands might find new customers to become included in this group. Ignoring them in marketing efforts might mean you lose their repeat business.

- Loyalty programs, while extremely popular with marketers, have shown to be ineffective in boosting sales. Ploys like price drops tend to provide a temporary boost, with activity leveling out when the promotions are over.

Knowing this, how might you approach your branding strategy differently? What customers are you losing by omission? Maybe your new fan base is located right in the New Heartland and would be happy to lend their ears if you were to include them in your message.

In Part One of this book, we introduce you to the New Heartland. Not only will you understand where the New Heartland is geographically, but also where it is culturally. You'll get to know a bit about our lifestyle and beliefs. We'll talk about some common stereotypes and why they need to be blown up or celebrated. Because to learn how to Speak American,™ you must understand us first.

PART ONE

NEW HEARTLAND

=

POWERFUL

CULTURAL

SEGMENT

CHAPTER

1

MEET THE NEW HEARTLAND

Welcome to the New Heartland! We're a diverse group of mixed ethnicities, backgrounds, and interests. Not every-one listens to country music, lives on a farm, or picks their momma up at the train station after she gets out of prison.

Stretching from the Florida shores to the plains of North Dakota to the tumbleweeds of Texas, we cover quite a large area of the country. Though we have a great variety of individuals, there is a strong common thread that ties us together. It might be our faith, dedication to our local communities, or devotion to our families. It's highly likely that it's all of these and more. These are a few of the things that shape this region and help form its unique identity.

One thing you should take away from this book is that it's the culture, the values, and the lifestyle that sets the New Heartland apart.

Just keep repeating this mantra: It's a way of life, not a demographic. It's a way of life, not a demographic.

Don't rely solely on your insights team to direct the rationale for your New Heartland strategy. Those campaigns are easy to spot. Instead, factor their findings into a broader view of approaching this unique segment.

We'll share plenty of facts and figures that support the ideas presented in this book, but the numbers tell only part of the story. We are white-collar professionals and blue-collar factory workers. We are genteel old-money socialites and stay-at-home suburban soccer moms. We are fourth-generation tobacco farmers and city-dwelling workaholics. We are millionaires in mansions and inner-city welfare recipients. We drive old pickup trucks, new BMWs, and an eco-friendly Prius or two. We grab a quick bite to eat at Taco Bell for lunch and savor a glass of fine wine at a five-star restaurant at dinner time. We are conservative, liberal, rich, poor, white, black, Latino, Christian, Muslim, Jewish, and just about everything in between.

In that way, we are no different than the rest of the country.

But what we do have in common is what makes us distinctly different—our core values. It's worthy of mentioning again, that while our values are certainly not unique to the New Heartland, they are more deeply rooted here. They're more at the surface and discussed openly.

OUR CORE VALUES

In all of my conversations across the New Heartland, I heard several examples of core values, including honesty, hard work, loyalty, and love of country. But three were repeated over and over: Faith, Community, and Family.

These three pillars are a big deal and the root of our choices big and small. In our research with U.S. consumers, we found that, overall, 41 percent of consumers said they are more likely to buy products and services if the commercials and ads appeal to their core values. It appears that advertisers aren't yet hitting the mark here as in the same group of responders, only 4 percent said commercials and ads "often" appeal to their core values, while 42 percent said these ads

$$ BUYING BEHAVIOR $$

FAITH
COMMUNITY
FAMILY

CORE VALUES AND BUYING BEHAVIOR IN THE NEW HEARTLAND

Illustration 1

"rarely" appeal to their core values. New Heartlanders specifically find messages that appeal to faith, friends, and family to be more effective than non-New Heartlanders do.[3]

These three core values are essential to brand success in the New Heartland. They're the foundation of our culture and the basis on which we make our decisions. From the types of movies we see to the cars we buy, these values are part of the selection process. If you'd like to get to know us, this is the first place to start.

WHERE IS THE NEW HEARTLAND?

"What's so new about the New Heartland?," you might be asking yourself. When most people think of the Heartland, they only include the traditional "flyover" states in the Midwest. Throughout my research, it became very clear that values common in the New Heartland were embedded in a much larger geographic footprint than the Midwest, hence the "New" Heartland.

NEW HEARTLAND STATES

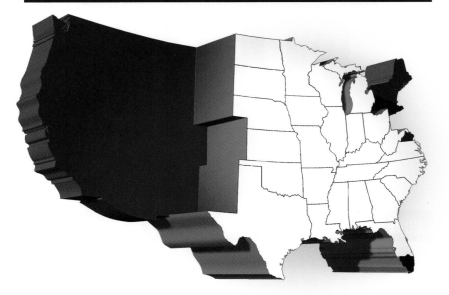

As much as the New Heartland is defined by a shared set of values, culture, and lifestyles, we still need to set up some parameters to distinguish the geographical location.

Our division of states is an extremely important factor in understanding the population on a local level. Our elected officials and state laws are large indicators of the issues most important to a community. It also helps us study data on the economic behaviors and areas of interest particular to a certain region. And let's face it, Americans across the country have a lot of state pride. Our home states often help shape our belief structures. For some (Texans, I'm looking at you), it can even be a part of our identity. One of my best high school friends was born in Texas. Even though he grew up in Memphis, he always proudly pulled out the "I'm a Texan" label when he was trying to act tough.

The accents vary greatly, but the ideals and lifestyles can be strikingly similar. Large land areas and flat, fertile earth make the perfect place for an agricultural economy and an outdoor lifestyle. How does that shape our behavior as a consumer? The three core values pillars previously mentioned have a lot to do with it. The sense of community derived from past generations that needed the help of the collective to raise and sell crops is a shared trait. The expansive land areas provide opportunity for common interests, such as hunting and camping. And the faith that the early settlers instilled in the areas continues to be very strong in these regions.

The United States Census Bureau lists the midwestern states as Wisconsin, Michigan, Illinois, Indiana, Ohio, Missouri, North Dakota, South Dakota, Nebraska, Kansas, Minnesota, and Iowa. For the South, it names Delaware (really?), Maryland, District of Columbia, Virginia, West Virginia, North Carolina, South Carolina, Georgia, Florida, Kentucky, Tennessee, Mississippi, Alabama, Oklahoma, Texas, Arkansas, and Louisiana.

I would largely agree that most of these states are included in what I call the New Heartland, with respect to their lifestyle and ideals. There are a few exceptions, though, that we should address. Florida, Delaware, Maryland, Virginia, and even Washington D.C. warrant a further look. Let's consider these individually to determine if they need to be included.

District of Columbia

The District of Columbia was established in 1790 as the capital of the United States, built on lands shared by Maryland and Virginia, two traditionally southern states. But politically and ideologically, it has mostly sided with the North. During the Civil War, the city continued to serve as the capital of the Union after the South seceded, giving it a firm historical claim as a northern city more than 150 years ago.

Today, Washington D.C. is a very diverse city of more than six hundred thousand that swells to well over one million during the day. Given the national and international nature of the federal government, a good portion of people that live and work in D.C. at any given time are actually from another state or country. It has become such a mix of cultures and nationalities that it retains little of the southern attributes or New Heartland personality. It lost the charm that it might have had when it was still part of the very rural Virginia and Maryland. Washington D.C. didn't make the New Heartland cut.

Florida

Most of Florida sits squarely in the middle of my New Heartland definition. The exception would be the southeast region, stretching from Palm Beach down to the Keys. Like D.C., this area shares little of the New Heartland lifestyle found in the rest of the region, as many of its residents aren't from there. Miami you'll find to be quite the international city with more than one-half (58 percent) of the residents born in another country, according to the most recent U.S. census. Palm Beach County and Boca Raton are also home to many retirees from around the country. While this influx of transports certainly adds to the rich and unique melting pot that is Florida, it does little to retain the values of the New Heartland.

So Florida is in, but I'm shading the southeastern portion out.

Delaware and Maryland

Eight-term North Carolina Senator Hamilton C. Horton Jr. might have best summed up how to tell if you were in southern territory. If presented with the question "Are you a Southerner?" and you replied "Hell, yes!" then you were from down in Dixie. You see, Southerners are a proud sort and are eager to claim the region, so answering in the affirmative put you south of the "Hell, yes!" line.

The place where you claim to be from does say a lot about how you identify yourself. If you don't claim southern heritage, you probably don't align with the culture either. Both of these states have stronger ties to Washington D.C. than the South, so we won't count them among our New Heartland states.

21

Virginia

There is no doubt that this state has Southern pride. Well, part of it anyway. You might think the Mason-Dixon Line runs right through the middle, if you talked to residents in the north and south. Again, Virginia has a lot of feeder communities to the capital. Those extra four hundred thousand a day have to come from somewhere! According to *Forbes*, the counties of Arlington, Fairfax, Loudoun, and Prince William have gone from being suburbs of D.C. to actually becoming a new metropolitan area in their own right.

The expanding federal government no doubt plays a large part in the area's growth; the Central Intelligence Agency and the Department of Defense are headquartered there, and it is home to many other government agencies. The area also has one of the largest technology industries outside of Silicon Valley. Northern Virginia has one of the most affluent and educated populations in the country; an astonishing 35 percent of Arlington County's population, for example, hold a graduate or professional degree.

Affluence and big business alone do not discount an area from being in the New Heartland. Just look at Chicago and Atlanta. But it is clear that this area is virtually part of and highly influenced by the D.C. metro area and has more in common with its counterpart across the Potomac than it does with, say, Roanoke or Norfolk.

For our purposes, Delaware, Maryland, Washington D.C., northern Virginia, and southeastern Florida are not part of the New Heartland.

DEBUNKING AND CELEBRATING THE STEREOTYPES

Every region, race, gender, and age is stereotyped to some extent. White guys can't jump; black guys are good athletes; women can't drive; and country folks are backward hicks. Good or bad, right or wrong, offensive or not, stereotyping is part of human nature.

A major frustration throughout my career has been the negative stereotypes of the New Heartland consumer that many agencies and brand managers on the coasts seem to easily accept, if not perpetuate. This pervasive bias prevents brand managers, a generally creative and inspired group, from recognizing the value of building relationships with this segment.

Once we overcome our natural tendency to stereotype, we quickly learn that nothing applies to everybody. Period. This includes my take on Madison Avenue's way of approaching marketing to the New Heartland. Not everyone dismisses this group. There are insightful brand managers and a creative director or two who understand or attempt to understand the New Heartland's idiosyncrasies.

However, the reality is, most do not. Let's address them head on. To get more specific about outside opinions concerning the New Heartland, I called on some of my colleagues from the East and West Coasts. I asked for a few words, phrases, or sentences that they felt described the New Heartland. I asked for honesty in exchange for anonymity, and, boy, did I get it:

> *"Nothing but cornfields."*

> *"Country bumpkin, little/no makeup, calico print dresses & boots."*

> *"Not as educated."*

> *"Closed-minded, slow, not aware of current events and politics."*

"They don't celebrate 'culture' per se."

"People in the New Heartland are political and religious conservatives; they watch Fox News and actually believe its claim to be 'fair and balanced;' they listen to conservative AM radio talk shows like Rush Limbaugh; they are actually racist but don't realize it because they have only been around white people who are like them; they eat a horrible diet of fatty, sugary empty calories; they always vote Republican; they listen to country music exclusively; they go to mega-churches with pastors that pander to greed and self-righteous attitudes."

"Somewhat poor, boring, average intelligence, farmers. Very 'average' American."

"Rednecks, bigots, gun racks."

Even if this isn't your personal view, is it how your agency views the New Heartland? Or your creative team? Or your client? Or your media buyer? It's worth finding out.

How about some facts and figures to help debunk a few stereotypes. I can talk about core values, personal interviews, and my own experiences until I'm blue in the face, and for some of you, that just won't be enough. You're a "numbers person." This section is for you.

In the geographic area we've outlined, according to the most recent U.S. government census report, New Heartland residents total *170 million* strong. That's nearly 60 percent of the nation. Even though we might be more spread out in certain areas, we account for a majority of the population.

"NOTHING BUT CORNFIELDS"

We also account for a majority of large cities. Of the largest twenty cities in terms of population, we claim thirteen. The coasts might have New York and Los Angeles, but we have Chicago, Houston, Dallas, San Antonio, Columbus, Indianapolis, Jacksonville, Austin, Charlotte, and others. Surprised they're in the top twenty? These New Heartland cities are all bigger than places such as Denver, Washington D.C., Seattle, and Las Vegas.

Don't get me wrong; we love our farms and have millions of acres dedicated to raising crops and livestock. We're not called "America's Breadbasket" for nothing. But we're not the only farmers in the country. This vast nation is full of farms in every corner. Ever traveled into the heart of New Jersey, out to Suffolk County, or across those hills that surround L.A.? Plenty of farms. In fact, according to the U.S. Department of Agriculture, the New Heartland states have more than 614 million acres of farmland[4], while the rest of the states still claim more than 592 million. While we clearly have more rows to hoe, the rest of the country is pretty close in the workload.

"NOT AS EDUCATED"

When we're not working the fields, we're busy running the boardrooms. Our success is proven in the numbers. In the Fortune 500 list, seven of the top ten[5] companies were based in the New Heartland. In fact, most of the companies on the entire list were ours—280! *Forbes* also recently named six New Heartland cities in a top-ten

TOP 10 FORTUNE 500 COMPANIES

1 Wal-Mart Stores	6 Phillips 66
2 Exxon Mobil	7 General Motors
3 Chevron	8 Ford Motor
4 Berkshire Hathaway	9 General Electric
5 Apple	10 Valero Energy

Illustration 2

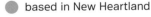 based in New Heartland

TOP 10 CITIES FOR INFORMATION JOBS

1 San Jose, CA	6 Atlanta, GA
2 San Francisco, CA	7 San Antonio, TX
3 Boston, MA	8 Raleigh, NC
4 Austin, TX	9 Phoenix, AZ
5 Madison, WI	10 Nashville, TN

Illustration 3

● New Heartland cities

list[6] of best cities for information jobs. The information industry has long been a darling of the media—no surprise since the media constitutes a major part of this economic sector, which includes publishing, software, entertainment, and data processing.

"THEY DON'T CELEBRATE 'CULTURE' PER SE."

The statement above makes me wonder how the commenter defines "culture." With music alone, the South is responsible for the creation of rock and roll, blues, jazz, and country. Chicago gave us house music and Detroit, techno. The cultural influence didn't end there— it continues today. Country music is the number-one-selling genre across the nation. On *Billboard*'s annual Money Maker, the top two earners on the 2014 list were in the country genre—Taylor Swift and Kenny Chesney[7]. So, you can see that we not only start cultural movements, but we finish them as well.

True, the fashion and movie industries are located in New York and L.A. But it appears as if we've got a few states that have their eye on the silver screen, and they're doing a particularly good job at building film industries of their own. Christina Cassidy of the Associated Press reported, "A survey last year found that California lost $3 billion in wages from 2004 to 2011 because of film and TV production moving to other states and countries, according to a report in the *Los Angeles Times*. Half the wages went to states such as Georgia, North Carolina, and Louisiana that offer tax incentives and rebates to the industry."[8]

Georgia in particular is pushing its film industry aspirations with its reported five major studio developments and expansions in the coming years. The Motion Picture Association of America found that the state is responsible for $1.6 billion in wages.[9] Its plans to build a $90 million studio, entertainment facility, and campus on 2,800 acres near Savannah will give the state the biggest studio in the country.[10] But no need to wait for that studio to produce pop culture phenomena, as recent Georgia productions *The Walking Dead* and *The Hunger Games: Catching Fire* are doing just that.

"THEY EAT A HORRIBLE DIET OF FATTY, SUGARY EMPTY CALORIES."

The United States is undoubtedly having a problem with obesity levels. And it's true that Mississippi, Louisiana, and Arkansas have the highest obesity rates in the country, each with around 34 percent of its population considered medically obese.[11]

However, beyond those three states and the enviably healthy and lean Colorado, we're all in the same boat—not obese, but a little on the hefty side.

I'll admit, I've seen a lot of overweight people as I've driven throughout the New Heartland on my research mission. But I have seen many more people in a healthy weight range who make a conscious effort to stay fit. Even in the high-obesity states, there's still 65 percent of the population that is *not* obese. Glass half full!

A recently released study by the Center for Disease Control and Prevention actually found obesity rates declining in young children across the country.[12] In fact, Mississippi, a former top contender for the highest overweight levels in the nation, actually posted the highest decline at more than 13 percent in elementary schools. Whether Michelle Obama's work is showing some results or American families are making better choices for their children, this could be a great sign of things to come.

Our country's high obesity rate is a major issue and a threat to both our health and our economy. But as a brand marketer, don't make blanket assumptions based on a minority of the population. There are millions of New Heartland residents who have a healthy lifestyle and are very interested in brands that help them live that way.

So what do these facts and figures tell you? Well, it's just scratching the surface in painting a more accurate picture of the New Heartland consumer. But we all know that numbers are only part of the equation when you're trying to get to know a person and what drives them to buy a particular product.

"REDNECKS, BIGOTS, GUN RACKS."

New Heartlanders have a special way of owning a stereotype—at least some of them. And I must say, we're proud of quite a few. "The Bible Belt" is not an insult as much as it is a fact. The number of churches is staggering as every congregation wants to get it right. Southern hospitality is a phrase we love and practice. We expect our kids to say "Yes, ma'am" and "Yes, sir" the same way we say it. How great is it to be known for being friendly? And we will own the heck out of being a redneck—on our terms.

We've reclaimed "redneck" as a term of endearment that all at once signifies independence and an adventurous spirit with a little outlaw thrown in for good measure.

The word, originally used to define poor, suntanned farmers, became associated with any rural person of lower class, whether measured by wealth and/or ideology. This group, largely raised in the countryside, had a different set of available entertainment options than urban dwellers. Instead of attending museums and theaters, they might race cars or go honky-tonkin' (listening to live music). As you might guess, there's a different sort of energy level between an impromptu drag race and an art opening. This sort of wild abandon added a colorful characteristic to the term "redneck." It's also what we love most about the term. Have you ever gone four-wheeling in a mud pit ... at night? It's a great time. You'll quickly learn why it's pretty fun to be a part of this group.

That said, we understand the implications of the term "redneck" when called one by an outsider. In that context, it's usually not a compliment. The intent is to categorize us as ignorant, low class, and common. So, it's not a term I suggest you use. This is sort of an insider's club. If you want to self-identify as a redneck, you do it with pride. But if you call us one, best of luck to you. I would not want to be you if someone goes redneck on you.

There are also great stereotypes about the New Heartland. Here's a quote mentioned earlier in this chapter from one of my coast-based colleagues who had a bit of a mixed viewpoint.

> "When I think of the New Heartland, I think of home-cooked meals, good old-fashioned values, kind people who look out for their neighbors, and a place where you can still leave your doors unlocked (maybe not anymore). It's a slower pace, and they like it!"

We are known for our slower pace of life, strong community sense, and dedication to family. That's great. We'll own that.

I heard the same sentiments from New Heartland residents I interviewed.

"Living in the New Heartland, to me, is all about quality of life and being able to raise my kids with values. I have a great career, but I work with people that appreciate the value of family and free time, so we don't work ourselves to death."

— Guidance counselor from Tennessee

We're also known to be pretty welcoming people. Besides "Southern hospitality," "Minnesota nice" is one you may be familiar with. It isn't just an outdated phrase, either. This stereotype has quantifiable proof. A recent survey titled "Civic Life in America: Key Findings on the Civic Health of the Nation," released by the Corporation for National and Community Service, found that Minnesotans might just be friendlier than the rest of the nation. In the study, 65 percent of the nation claimed to help out neighbors in need, while that number rose to 71 percent in Minnesota. They also report that an amazing 88 percent of residents talk to their neighbors regularly. And while the Federal Agency for Service and Volunteering shows that the Midwest has the highest volunteer rates in the nation at 30 percent participation, Minnesota beats that at 38 percent. It's a nice place to be, for sure.

All stereotypes aren't bad, but the thing you as a marketer need to be aware of is not letting those stereotypes stand in the way of incorporating the New Heartland into your strategy.

30

KEY POINTS: MEET THE NEW HEARTLAND

» The New Heartland should be considered a cultural segment made up of an ethnically diverse set of Americans, sharing a common set of core values that influence our decisions and loyalties.

» The three most prominent values are Faith, Community, and Family.

» Geographically, the New Heartland consists of twenty-six states in the southeastern, southwestern and midwestern portions of America, omitting the metro areas of southern Florida, northern Virginia and Washington D.C.

» Speaking American is about being culturally relevant. Get to know this powerful cultural segment. Rely on trusted sources to get beyond your personal beliefs and stereotypes to round out the thinking for the benefit of your brand.

CHAPTER

2 FAITH ...
NOT RELIGION

FAITH
AND ITS IMPACT ON BUYING BEHAVIOR

74% OF AMERICANS IDENTIFY THEMSELVES AS **CHRISTIAN**

55% OF AMERICANS SAY **FAITH** IS A VERY IMPORTANT ASPECT OF THEIR LIVES

11 OF THE **TOP 12** MOST RELIGIOUS STATES ARE IN THE NEW HEARTLAND

NEW HEARTLANDERS + FAITH

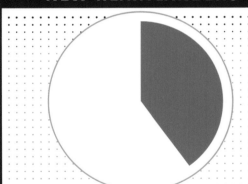

30% more likely to ATTEND CHURCH REGULARLY

40% more likely to find FAITH CRITICALLY IMPORTANT WHEN PURCHASING

21% MORE LIKELY TO CLAIM FAITH AS A VERY IMPORTANT CORE VALUE

40% more likely to find FAITH A VERY EFFECTIVE ADVERTISING ELEMENT

As I prepared to write my first book, a friend of mine who was a brand manager at Procter & Gamble (P&G) strongly cautioned me to stay away from using the word "faith." His position was that it was too offensive and polarizing.

But I disagree. It's the perfect word.

Faith ... not religion.

It describes believing in something much bigger than yourself, trusting it to be true, whether that's God or a moral code. The ability to believe in something wholeheartedly is life-changing. And to have an entire region describe it as one of their defining core values? Now, that's inspiring.

FAITH AND THE NEW HEARTLAND

A 2014 NBC/WSJ poll shows that 21 percent of respondents said that religion is "not that important" to their lives, compared to 16 percent who said the same thing in 1999.[13] The poll showed that these less-religious Americans are more likely to be men, have an income of more than $75,000, live in the Northeast or West, and be under the age of thirty-five.

However, in the same poll, 55 percent of Americans still place a major emphasis on their faith, saying religion is the most important or a very important aspect of their lives.

Posting some of the strongest poll numbers in the nation, it's quite evident that faith plays a large role in our everyday lives. The fact is that Christianity is the most-practiced *form* of faith in the U.S.—but it's certainly not the only one.

A recent Gallup Poll found that 74 percent of the country's population identify themselves as Christian. Here's the breakdown of America's top religious affiliations:[14]

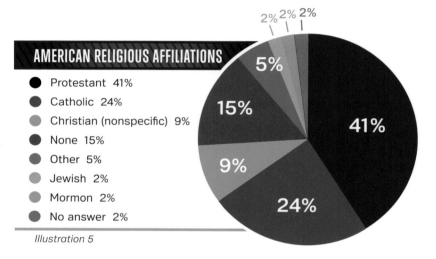

AMERICAN RELIGIOUS AFFILIATIONS

● Protestant 41%
● Catholic 24%
● Christian (nonspecific) 9%
● None 15%
● Other 5%
● Jewish 2%
● Mormon 2%
● No answer 2%

Illustration 5

The largest number of churchgoers can be found in the New Heartland. Of the top-ranked states found to be the most religious, the New Heartland has nine of them, and includes none in the bottom ten. As the Gallup Map in Illustration 6 shows, you'll find us in the pews on Sunday morning.[15]

So, we're faithful people, at least on the surface. It's a stereotype that's mostly true. Being faithful doesn't mean we're politically or socially conservative as the stereotype says we are. It just means we rely on our faith in good times and the bad. But how does that factor into our daily choices?

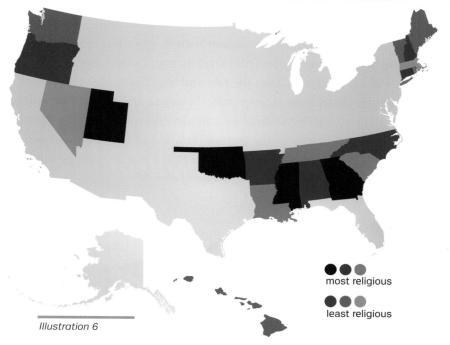

MOST RELIGIOUS STATES BY CHURCH ATTENDANCE

● ● ● most religious

● ● ● least religious

Illustration 6

According to our own New Heartland Consumer Insights Study, 45 percent of New Heartlanders surveyed say faith is somewhat or critically important to them when making purchasing decisions, and 44 percent say that faith as an advertising element is an effective means of getting them to purchase.[16] This could apply to the values of the company, the tone of the advertising campaign, or the product itself. New Heartland residents need to have faith in not only your product, but your company as well.

In my travels around the New Heartland, I met people of all backgrounds, incomes, ethnicities, religions, and races. Regardless of their differences, nine out of ten mentioned their faith as a core value, and took the time to carefully explain its importance. It became clear that faith is a way of life to these people, and it has a strong impact on many of the decisions they make.

Even faith-based programming is finding success. Apparently, NBC has had a "Come to Jesus" moment with its purchase of *The Bible*, an overnight hit miniseries from The History Channel that depicted a sort of Greatest Hits from the Old and New Testaments. The first episode garnered more than 13 million viewers, and held strong with more than 11 million in the season finale. The success of *The Bible* led to the production of the feature film, *Son of God*, co-produced by reality TV czar Mark Burnett. *Son of God* was a hit, scoring more than $26 million on its opening weekend alone.[17]

Burnett, whose smash shows include *Shark Tank*, *Survivor*, and *The Voice*, and his wife, former *Touched by an Angel* star Roma Downey, produced the new *Son of God* movie, which depicts the life and death of Jesus Christ.

"I will tell you there are a lot of Christians who love Jesus, who love God in Hollywood," Burnett told *The Steve Malzberg Show* on Newsmax TV.

"I've got news for everybody out there," he said. "Hey, the mass of Americans love family-friendly, love God. It's one nation under God. Get over it."

FAITH AND BRANDS

You probably already had a good idea how big faith was in the New Heartland, but you might still be wondering what that means for your brand.

As part of our core values, faith has a huge role in our everyday decisions, big or small. From whom we marry to the brands we buy, faith is a major influence on those decisions. And we're certainly not afraid to openly discuss and in many cases (but not all), practice it.

It's not uncommon to be a part of workplace Bible studies, student-led prayer groups, and blessings said before an event or meal. Yet, despite the New Heartland's willingness and even enthusiasm for discussing faith, most brands have avoided acknowledging the role that it plays in our lives. Brand marketers sweep faith under the rug as if it were not important or just too complex to deal with.

*Your brand doesn't need to pander to faith-based groups. The brand team and the creative team need to be aligned on the **role** faith plays in buying behavior with New Heartland consumers. Be smart with the creative. It can still be funny and irreverent.*

Yes, faith is complex. But it also has to be dealt with at a strategic level. While brands that ignore faith might be appeasing the nonbelievers, just 15 percent of Americans, mind you—they run the risk of seriously offending the faithful, which represents the vast majority of our country. Unfortunately, many of the people I talked to have become accustomed to companies discounting their faith and treating them as backwoods bumpkins because of their strong beliefs. Trust me, they resent it.

An example of this is the annual holiday question: Can we say Christmas? Every year, the media will tout "The War on Christmas." And as we will undoubtedly roll our eyes because we know that Christmas still dominates the season; there has to be a reason that so many people are rightfully upset.

As we know, Christmas celebrates the birth of Christ. It is the biggest Christian holiday. In past decades, as the celebration became more commercialized and retailers took advantage of the biggest shopping season of the year, the face of the holiday largely changed from Jesus to Santa Claus. This switch is a huge hit to the very spirit of Christmas. So, for the media and some brands to tell us that we shouldn't even include the word 'Christmas' to refer to the holiday? Well, it just seems ridiculous.

Don't get me wrong, we love all of the symbols of Christmas, religious or not. The lights, caroling, trees, shopping—all of it gives us a way to celebrate one of our favorite religious holidays. And we are even fine  with people who want to celebrate the day without the religious connotations. It just seems curious why brands won't acknowledge the holiday that accounts for their biggest annual sales numbers. It is, in fact, Christmas that we're celebrating. Why is it so taboo to mention that?

Not all brands shy away from faith, however. Many large brands include faith-rooted beliefs in mission statements, office culture, advertising campaigns, or even on brand packaging. In-N-Out Burger prints Bible verses on their fast food containers. Forever 21 does the same on their shopping bags and some clothing items.

This practice does not solely apply to Christianity. In a *Fast Company* profile, Timberland CEO Jeff Swartz discussed how his Jewish faith guided him in making a decision to relocate product production away from a Chinese company that didn't align with his moral beliefs. He said, "I have a religious feeling that guides me. I can't show you the scripture that relates to the rights of a worker, but I can show you text that insists upon treating others with dignity. It says in the Hebrew Bible one time that you should love your neighbor as yourself, but it says dozens of times that you shall treat the stranger with dignity." Should Swartz have omitted the reason he made a game-changing decision that affected the entire company because it involved his faith? Absolutely not! The move gained him more supporters for his ethically responsible decision, and surely didn't upset customers due to the role faith played in it.

So, what does this mean for your brand? Should you write up a faith-based mission statement, build a company chapel, and include Jesus quotes on your employee's paychecks? Not necessarily. What this does mean is that you should decide, and make known, what is important to you, your brand, and your customers.

If faith plays a large role in your company culture and business decisions, your customers might like to know that. We've already discussed how much faith plays a role in purchasing decisions, so letting consumers know that your beliefs align with theirs can be a good thing.

Just be wary of trying to please everybody, because that's impossible. The make-everyone-happy strategy was employed by GAP a few years ago when they paid a lighthearted tribute to several wintertime holidays when they ran a TV commercial with this jingle:

Go Christmas, Go Hanukkah, Go Kwanzaa, Go solstice!
Go Christmas, Go Hanukkah, Go whatever holiday you
Wannakuh!

What was probably meant to be a message of inclusion, instead came off as flippant and dismissive of the holidays' various religious connotations. It's not a strategy I would advise.

Brands can also go too far the other way as well, and try so hard to not offend that it becomes ridiculous. Another Christmastime faux pas saw Hallmark in the hot seat. In their line of annual signature Christmas Tree ornaments, they released a miniature sweater with a line from the song "Deck the Halls" printed on the front. They took the liberty of changing the stanza from "Don we now our gay apparel," to "Don we now our FUN apparel!" This angered some customers as they felt that the message the card company was sending was that "gay" was an offensive term.

Hallmark responded to the outcry, attempting to explain their position. "When the lyrics to 'Deck the Halls' were translated from Gaelic and published in English back in the 1800s, the word 'gay' meant festive or merry," said Hallmark's Kristi Ernsting. "Today it has multiple meanings ... the trend of wearing festively decorated Christmas sweaters to parties is all about fun, and this ornament is intended to play into that, so the planning team decided to say what we meant: 'fun.'"

While Hallmark was correct to respond publicly to their upset customers, they were off the mark in their reply. Their subsequent statement is the one that should have been said first. "We've been surprised at the wide range of reactions expressed about the change of lyrics on this ornament, and we're sorry to have caused so much concern. We never intend to offend or make political statements with our products, and in hindsight, we realize we shouldn't have changed the lyrics on the ornament."

If their creative team hadn't been over concerned with offending people in the first place, there would have never been the need to apologize.

It may seem that a brand can't win here. But this isn't hard. If you respect your customers' beliefs and are transparent about your own, you'll more than likely earn respect from people of many different convictions.

Former P&G chief marketing officer and branding expert Jim Stengel wrote a great book called *Grow*. He and his team did a ten-year study to determine the correlation between a company's ideals and its growth. "A company's ideals are the ultimate driver of growth," Stengel writes.

He goes on to say, "Many leaders intuitively understand that their businesses and brands need a higher purpose

JIM STENGEL'S FIVE FIELDS OF FUNDAMENTAL HUMAN VALUES

1. *Eliciting Joy*
2. *Enabling Connection*
3. *Inspiring Exploration*
4. *Evoking Pride*
5. *Impacting Society*

in order to have a more important place in people's lives than the competition. They just don't know how to judge whether they have positioned their businesses and brands in the right space." To help leaders make that judgment, he developed five areas of fundamental human values. The five fields "give you an acid test for gauging the validity and growth potential of an ideal, and show whether you are aiming high enough and have a chance of engaging people at the level of their most-profound concerns, needs, beliefs, and values."

Faith and brands can coexist as long as the relationship is genuine and the message is clear.

What about your brand? Is it founded on principles with which your customers can relate? You might find that sharing your ideals provides an opportunity for your customers to connect on a deeper level with your brand.

If your brand finds a way to authentically partner with personalities such as the Robertson family on *Duck Dynasty* that isn't shy about their faith, be prepared to stand firm on what your brand represents. Weak brands are exposed in the face of controversy.

Being open about your brand's core beliefs can be a great way to find common ground with the New Heartland.

Duck Dynasty Brands with Faith

For those of you unfamiliar with the phenomenon that is the *Duck Dynasty* television program, let me introduce you to the Robertson clan. This reality TV show about a Louisiana family that built an empire designing and selling duck calls, is breaking cable television records and creating superstars of some very colorful family members. The show depicts the daily lives of the Robertson men—Phil and Si, and Phil's three sons Jase, Willie, and Jep—as well as their wives and children.

As reality TV shows usually promise, you're entertained by the hijinks of a unique subculture of characters, and in this, *Duck Dynasty* definitely delivers. The men are famous for their long beards, camouflage attire, and ingenuity. One episode might see them transforming a pond into a "redneck water park," complete with a rope swing and a trampoline floating on inner tubes. Another show might feature the boys tricking out an old trailer to hoist up into the trees as a duck blind. Yes, this is stereotypical country living to the core, and they're proud of it.

Like most New Heartlanders, the Robertsons are not afraid to show their strong faith. A family prayer and dinner scene has become the signature sign-off for every episode. With the highest ratings posting in southern states, it's apparent that the ideals align with the people of the New Heartland.

The Robertsons' religious views aren't confined to the television program, however. They speak openly in interviews and at organized events about their faith as well. Frequent paid appearances around the country sell out in hours. The talks center around the show, their business, and their faith. Resembling more of a sermon than a duck call demonstration, the family makes sure that you know who they thank for their success. And with Phil Robertson's estimate that they receive about six hundred speaking invites a day, the message seems to be resonating pretty well.

CASE STUDY

The Robertsons have a massive brand to protect. They currently have one of the top-rated unscripted shows on cable. The 2013 season premiere brought in an astounding 11.8 million viewers. They have two No. 1 *New York Times* best-selling books, two multimillion dollar companies (Duck Commander and Buck Commander), a myriad of memorabilia, and upcoming releases for DVDs, books, and even an album. Everything from garden gnomes to lunch boxes bear their likeness. Yet even with so much invested in so many properties, the family doesn't shy away from sharing their Christian faith.

That core value of faith in the Duck Dynasty brand was tested by fire. In a bizarre string of events, the family's patriarch Phil Robertson was suspended from the A&E program after remarks he made in a *GQ* article regarding something which he believed was sinful. After an outcry from the public in support of Robertson, the network apologized to the fans and put him back on the air.

So where did that controversy land the brand that stayed consistent to the core value of faith? CNBC reported on *Duck Dynasty* licensing and merchandising power after the Robertson comment, quoting Martin Brochstein, senior vice president of the International Licensing Industry Merchandisers Association, "It's pushing consumers to make *Duck Dynasty* purchases a personal vote on the Robertsons' beliefs. It now makes it a conscious cultural choice. And in the meantime, while we wait to see if retail sales wane, the show is expected to continue to draw record viewers—its premiere last season drew nearly twelve million viewers, the most-watched cable nonfiction show ever."

By showing their authentic selves, the Robertsons were able to make a connection with viewers in the New Heartland and around the nation. In celebrating their faith instead of hiding it, they have only seen their brand grow.

» Faith (not necessarily religion) has a huge impact on New Heartlanders' decisions and actions, so disregarding their beliefs or offending this group can be a big misstep in developing your brand.

» More than 80 percent of the country claims a religious affiliation, with Christianity comprising 96 percent of those believers. If faith plays a large role in the decisions of your company, chances are your customers will be able to appreciate and identify with that.

» Be wary of trying to please everybody as the result could be confusing and counterproductive.

» Make sure your creatives understand the role that faith plays in the New Heartland.

KEY POINTS: FAITH ... NOT RELIGION

CHAPTER

3 COMMUNITY

THE POWER OF **COMMUNITY**

92%

OF U.S. CONSUMERS trust recommendations from **FRIENDS AND FAMILY** ABOVE ANY OTHER TYPE OF ADVERTISING SOURCE

2/3
OF NATIONAL BRANDS invest in **LOCAL MARKETING EFFORTS** to connect with people in their hometown community

MORE THAN
70%
OF MIDWESTERN ADULTS live in their birth state because they want to stay where they grew up

SOCIAL **WORD OF MOUTH** increases marketing effectiveness up to **54%**

NEIGHBORS COMMUNITY VERY IMPORTANT IN PURCHASE DECISIONS

49% WOMEN

41% MEN

+

OFFLINE WOM has a **MORE SIGNIFICANT IMPACT** on buying outcomes than social media

64% of women said NEIGHBORS/COMMUNITY as an advertising element **motivates them to buy** $$$$$

86%
of New Heartland **WOMEN** find FRIENDS as an advertising element effective in influencing purchase.

Illustration 7

Communities take so many shapes and forms. They can exist online, in a church building, a YMCA, or your neighborhood, to name a few. Wherever they are, they're very strong in the New Heartland—and highly influential.

That's probably why nearly two-thirds of national brands invest in local marketing efforts to connect with people in their hometown community. In addition to advertising in local community newspapers (43 percent) and sending emails to local customers (37 percent), national brands now rely on social media to connect with local audiences. Facebook dominates the social community usage by brands[18] (58 percent) followed by Google (37 percent including Google+ and Google Maps).

% NATIONAL BRANDS USING LOCAL MARKETING

FACEBOOK	58%
LOCAL MEDIA	43%
EMAIL	37%
GOOGLE	37%

Illustration 8

But to fully grasp the importance of community in the New Heartland, it is important to understand that it's about more than just location. For most New Heartland towns, you could take the people and move them to an entirely new location and the community would be unchanged. Community is more about relationships and shared values than it is about geography.

COMMUNITY IS ABOUT RELATIONSHIPS

This kind of kinship can provide great opportunities for word-of-mouth marketing and building brand trust. It means favorite brands are being personally invited into their communities. And that's a top honor.

"Community" is a broad term to define in the New Heartland because it includes so many groups, with each one so vitally important. Here, the value of community goes hand-in-hand with faith and family. You'll find that most New Heartland communities are made up of an inextricable web of relationships—family is certainly at the heart of it often because so many extended families live within a close drive of each other.

There's also the church family, neighbors, coworkers, sports teams, and the myriad people you know through your kids, such as teachers and their friends' parents.

The end result: you really can't go to the grocery store in most New Heartland communities without seeing someone you know.

But you know what? I really enjoy that, most of the time. I don't mind that it takes me ten minutes longer to pick up something at Lowe's because I run into someone I know. Maybe it's just my personality type, but it's another New Heartland characteristic that agrees with me.

This community is more than just a place where I shop and pay my electric bills. It plays a big role in defining who I am and how my family fits in.

Community is such a big part of my life that I made a conscious decision to make sure we were deeply connected when we moved back to Nashville from a two-year stint with Elvis Presley Enterprises in Memphis. Instead of putting my business back on "Music Row" (close to downtown Nashville), I chose to rent office space very close to my house. Everything that's important to me is within a fifteen-minute radius: home, work, the kids' schools, and church. Nearly everything we do happens in the Brentwood/Franklin suburb of Nashville, and I couldn't be happier. My commute to my office is four minutes ... six minutes on a bad day! I'm convinced that the amount of angst I save from not commuting forty minutes downtown, as I did for seventeen years, has added years to my life.

In an article by David Hochman in *Readers Digest*, Harvard psychologist Daniel Gilbert discussed key elements to achieving true happiness in life, based on years of research. Many of the sources he brought to light are readily available and embraced by the New Heartland:

"Churchgoers are happier than non-churchgoers, but not for the reasons people expect. Our best indication is that it's not the religion part that makes people happy. It's the going-to-church part. *It's the community part.* It's the holding hands and singing. It's the knowing-folks-who-would-bring-you-soup-if-you-got-sick part."

Being a part of a tight-knit community can have a big impact on personal happiness. And we're quite a smiling group according to a fun experiment from the makers of a new city guide app Jetpac, a phone application that analyzes cities through Instagram photos, and can give you a more complete picture of a restaurant, trail, or neighborhood by the shots taken there.

Want to know which are the greenest parks or where the twenty-somethings are partying? You'll find it here. You'll also find out who seems to be having the best time. The Jetpac team demonstrated the app's abilities by releasing their findings on the top smile scores in the U.S.[19] The score is a measurement of just how big the grins are in the Instagram photos taken in each of the more than five thousand cities. St. Louis was found to be the merriest, followed by Kansas City, Missouri, and Columbus, Ohio. That's right, they're all New Heartland states. In fact, nine of the top ten were in the New Heartland. This is, of course, just a fun experiment from some very smart and creative developers, but a picture does say a thousand words.

TOP 10 HAPPIEST U.S. CITIES

1 ST. LOUIS, MO
2 KANSAS CITY, MO
3 COLUMBUS, OH
4 INDIANAPOLIS, IN
5 PITTSBURGH, PA
6 SAN ANTONIO, TX
7 MINNEAPOLIS, MN
8 JACKSONVILLE, FL
9 DETROIT, MI
10 RALEIGH, NC

Illustration 9   ● New Heartland

Many of the people I spoke with echoed my sentiments when they talked about the importance their community plays in their lives. A member of a country music group I interviewed pointed out that the "community is our family ... we were raised by our community."

This tight-knit mentality is a good reason why we tend to stick around as well. While there are always exceptions to the rule, it's true that we're more inclined to stay near our hometowns more than our coastal counterparts. Even among those who move away from home for school or work, many will eventually return home to settle down and have a family, or perhaps to retire, but many more never even leave. Just being a member of your community isn't enough, though. You'll easily find a helping hand in good and bad times. As a matter of fact, according to the Corporation for National & Community Service, the Midwest has the highest percentage of volunteers in the country with just more than 30 percent of people giving their time to help someone else.[20]

The latest census report finds, roots run deepest in the Midwest—more than 70 percent of all adults live in the same state in which they were born.[21] That compares with fewer than half of those who live in western states. We found in our New Heartland Consumer Insights Study that it's a common theme for the rest of the New Heartland as well. Here, 45 percent of New Heartland responders claim to live within a two-hour drive from most or all of their family members, compared to 39 percent of residents outside the New Heartland claiming the same.[22]

The reason they stay put? According to a study by the Pew Research Center, family is the biggest influence, cited by 74 percent.[23] Wanting to stay where they grew up comes in at 69 percent, and the belief that their hometown is a great place to raise their families was claimed by 59 percent.

Sound familiar? Family. Community. Faith. It's what the New Heartland is all about.

These stats are vitally important to brand builders. It illustrates the multiple levels of connections New Heartlanders have to their communities and why brand messaging needs to be relevant. Many times the messaging gets diluted or the New Heartland isn't accounted for in the creative process. This common disconnect causes big problems for brands who don't realize the missed opportunity. Brands need to work harder to uncover their true potential among a group of consumers that just want to be paid attention to in a believable way.

This isn't hard ... it just takes effort.

WORD OF MOUTH GOLD

Since community is defined here by not only the geographic location, but also the sets of relationships we share with each other, there are a few important ways for brands to engage the New Heartland. Our volunteer groups, youth sports, and families each have their own importance. They all make up pillars on which we base our decisions, big and small. So, you can imagine the power that Word of Mouth (WOM) plays.

The importance of building a brand through Word of Mouth can't be underestimated. Featured in an article in *Ad Age*, a study conducted by MarketShare proved that WOM has a direct link to driving sales.[24] They studied several different brands and found that social Word of Mouth increased marketing effectiveness up to 54 percent. Until this study, it was difficult to measure if what people say to each other about their brand experience has a direct effect on sales. We know WOM has a direct effect because we experience it ourselves in everyday life.

When we move to a new area, it's our neighbors and friends who recommend the dentist, doctor, best school, babysitter, etc. Services like Angie's List tapped right into that age-old need of finding services that were trustworthy and economical. I'm the kind of person who has "a guy" for nearly everything. I like to recommend my various guys for house painting, plumbing, electrical work, yard maintenance, and auto repairs ... you name it and I have a guy for it. I'm very loyal to the people and companies that take care of me, and I want to share my experiences with my friends so they don't have to learn the hard way.

TIPS FOR ENGAGING NEW HEARTLANDERS

1. *Target Influencers*
2. *Build a Close-knit Social Community*
3. *Be a Thought Leader*
4. *Always Be Honest*

If you want to be talked up in the New Heartland, there are some key practices you'll want to employ:

1. *Target Influencers:* Make sure you are speaking to leaders and influencers in your space. Choose experts from the New Heartland. Not only does it encourage a greater sense of trust to engage a local leader, but they will also be able to speak the area language as well as have a better sense of what's important to their constituents. These influencers can be journalists, public figures, bloggers, or even trendsetting fans. Make a target list of influencers who appeal to your target demographic, make sure that they buy into what you do, and that they reflect the brand vision. Take the time to learn about them and why they are influential, then open up a dialogue by engaging with their content and viewpoint in ways that are relevant to your brand. They will play a critical role in introducing and/or vouching for your brand in local circles and communities.

2. *Build a Close-knit Social Community:* This isn't earth-shattering news, but the easiest way to directly communicate with your audience is to engage with them via the *right* social platforms. Nearly every brand is in the social space, but few do a good job leveraging its power. A study conducted by Pew Research Centers in 2013 found that 73 percent of adult Internet users use social media.[25] Of all the American users on Facebook, 47 percent claim the social media site to be the top influencer on purchasing decisions. These sites provide a powerful way to directly connect with your customers in real time.

3. *Be a Thought Leader:* Not only do you want to target the influencers in your space, you want to be one! When you get the attention of the New Heartland, you want to show that you're an expert in your industry. Figure out what makes you and your business unique, and tell people about it. Determine the medium that best supports your ideas, and develop a strategy to

grow your presence there. Stop saying the same thing everyone else does in your space. Be real ... be authentic ... and speak American.

4. *Always be honest:* The success of Word of Mouth marketing depends on whether or not your customer trusts your brand. You have to earn enough merit to become a worthy topic of conversation. You can do this with an exceptional product, outstanding customer service, and maintaining integrity across all digital platforms. Honesty and transparency are mighty strong virtues in the New Heartland. So is asking for forgiveness when you screw up.

Before you can work on increasing your positive Word of Mouth among customers, you must first find out what people think about your brand.

When I speak at industry events, I try to gather Word of Mouth sentiments by getting the audience involved. Selfishly, I enjoy learning what they have to say about the topic about which I'm speaking. One successful tactic I've used to find out what they think about particular brands is doing a brand tag exercise, similar to the site brandtags. com. According to the site, "Brand Tags is a brand playground— the place for people to freely share their opinions about brands ... and where brand owners and agencies can access the unvarnished truth for free."

I show a brand logo, and then the audience calls out their gut reaction in a few words. One hundred percent of the time I've done a brand tag exercise during a presentation, it's matched up to the sentiments shared on the site. It's fascinating how brand sentiment is so consistent.

By understanding common sentiment about your brand, you'll have a better foundation on which to form strategies to enhance or change how consumers view your brand.

What happens if the feedback isn't good? Well, in the case of Ann Arbor-based Domino's, they owned it. This is an ad industry favorite and for good reason. The pizza chain was receiving terrible marks on their product.

"The crust tastes like cardboard."

"Microwave pizza is far superior."

"The sauce tastes like ketchup."

"It doesn't feel like there's much love in Domino's pizza."

These were just a few comments from among the many unsatisfied customers. Think about the old Word of Mouth adage here. "A customer who has a good experience will tell one person, yet a customer who has a bad experience will tell ten people." Can you imagine the damage that could be done here?

Rather than ignoring the complaints directed at them, Domino's listened and responded fantastically. They decided to completely remake their product. Domino's profits soared and so did public opinion.

You don't have to have a huge company to get a lot of buzz, however. Another Ann Arbor-based company generated plenty of WOM gold with their local effort as well.

CASE STUDY

Bank of Ann Arbor Becomes Neighborhood Friend

The Bank of Ann Arbor (BOAA) doesn't want your business, that is, unless you live in Ann Arbor. This Michigan bank opened only a few years ago and is already a town staple.

Posed with the question of how to get local residents to switch from their national banks, the people at BOAA came up with a creative solution in the form of billboard advertisements.

Crowd-sourced from more than seven hundred initial entries, the bank posted insider jokes on billboards around town. Suddenly, big national banks seemed like faceless behemoths while the Bank of Ann Arbor became your neighborhood friend that might know you by name.

Most all of the ads begin with "Non-local banks think" and end with some fun play on words that give residents a good chuckle, like "Ypsi is the guy who sings Gangnam Style" (it's an abbreviation of a nearby city) or "Community High is when we're all feeling really, really good." (It's a high school.)

You can bet these one-liners get plenty of conversations started around town.

The campaign, launched in 2009, helped the bank see an increase of $77 million in deposits and take it from the seventh-largest in the city, to the second-largest.

Their social media properties reflect their success as well. The bank has almost twenty-two thousand Facebook (FB) fans, an amazing feat for a local business. The FB content shows that they don't just reside in the town; they have an active participation in it as well. Pictures and videos are posted of their employees giving back to the community through

their time and monetary gifts. Even their newsfeed stays active with local news.

BOAA loves being a part of their community, and they do a great job of showing it. By participating in various volunteer organizations and charities, the bank is becoming a part of its neighbors' smaller communities. With their clever ads, they're thought of as the in-the-know, local bank. The Bank of Ann Arbor embraced the power of community, and as a result it enjoys incredible success.

» Communities are social and cultural intersections and can't be categorized just geographically.

» Even national or global brands need to think local ... don't underestimate the power of the local media, events, and social media communities to connect your brand with the New Heartlander.

» Word of Mouth drastically increases campaign effectiveness and brand advocacy. The New Heartland embraces and amplifies it more than any other cultural segment.

» Understanding why and how we form our communities is an essential part in learning how to gain access to them.

CHAPTER

4 FAMILY

FAMILY IS THE #1 SOURCE FOR PRODUCT RECOMMENDATIONS

70%

of consumers claim an opinion from a **FAMILY MEMBER IS THE MOST TRUSTED.**

▼

69% OF U.S. PARENTS CONSULT THEIR CHILDREN ON FAMILY PURCHASES

NEW HEARTLANDERS + FAMILY

62% MORE LIKELY AMONG WOMEN
VALUE INPUT OF FAMILY WHEN BUYING

81
SAY FAMILY IS A **VERY IMPORTANT CORE VALUE**

PERCENT

MORE MOTIVATED TO BUY BRANDS WHO USE **FAMILIES IN AD CAMPAIGNS**

79%

FAMILY IS A KEY BRAND INFLUENCER

Illustration 10

Our own personal little community that wields the most clout is family. Nearly every person I spoke with—single, married, with or without kids, young and old—echoed the sentiment that family is among their top priorities. Our own New Heartland Consumer Insights Study showed it as well with 81 percent of New Heartland responders claiming family to be a "very important" core value.[26]

The family unit, regardless of configuration, is the foundation of the New Heartlander's identity. Family plays a pivotal role in our lifestyle, purchasing habits, media consumption, technology use, priorities, and goals in life. As a Forrester Research report found, family is the number-one source for product recommendations, with 70 percent of responders claiming an opinion from a family member is the most trusted.[27] The whole family is in on the decision-making process as well. In the United States, a reported 69 percent of parents consult their children on family purchases.[28] So keeping a family-aware approach to your advertising isn't only good sense, it's good business.

If faith was the number-one core value I heard mentioned in my conversations with New Heartland consumers, then family was definitely a close second, if not a tie.

AMERICAN FAMILIES, TRADITIONS, AND BRANDS

For most of us, America is the most important brand. We love to buy American-made products. A recent look at Kelley Blue Book found that, in researching the most popular vehicles by each state, twenty-three of our twenty-six New Heartland states favored American-made cars, twenty-two of which were Fords.[29] This iconic U.S. company represents the values we revere, so it's no surprise that we'll keep their cars in our driveways for generations.

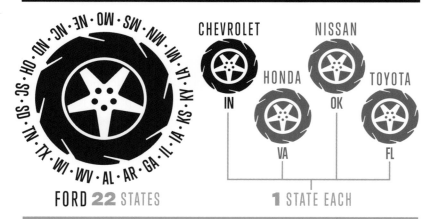

Illustration 11

The New Heartland is still one of the places where people today "seal a deal on a handshake."

My old Ford pick-up truck wasn't feeling well. I keep it at our lake house where it doesn't get a lot of attention. I called the local tow truck service in Smithville, Tennessee, to see if they'd pick it up and deliver it to the mechanic. They don't know me at all, so when I asked him how I would pay the $65 charge, he told me not to worry about it and "We'll work it out." Later that day, after he delivered the truck, he sent me a text with their address. I sent him a check the same day. That's just how business gets done down here.

There's an expectation of honest conduct and we reward that behavior with intense loyalty. This is true with our brand relationships as well. We expect brands to keep their promises.

After all, a brand is only as good as its word.

The important role of family is not exclusive to the New Heartland by any stretch, but it serves as the basis for molding individual ideals, core values, and communities. Hear it in the words of three New Heartland residents when asked about their core values:

> *"Providing for my wife, first of all, and then my kids, that's financially and spiritually. You want to make sure that your family is going to be taken care of if you're here or not. You want to give them everything you can. You want to keep them safe. You want to set an example, too. You want your kids to see who you are and then act that way when they finally grow up, so ... you hope they catch the right things and not the wrong things."*
> — Sales executive from Alabama

> *"I'm not married anymore, but I am a father and a grandpa. Family is more important than anything."*
> — Retired rodeo rider from Tennessee

> *"I love my God, I love my family, and I love my friends. I've got a pretty big family. I've got my mom and my sister and my nephew and my aunts and uncles and cousins that I talk to on a regular basis."*
> — College student in Tennessee

Family holds an undeniable link to our personal identity—many of our individual brand preferences and purchasing habits stem from family. Mothers make the same pie recipes as their moms did using the same ingredients. Sons grow up to drive the same brand of car as their dad. Parents and their grown children frequently shop together, vacation together, and now, live together.

Given the close proximity and frequent interaction, we tend to share interests and tastes. Our family traditions exert great influence over our patterns of behavior and perceptions of brand value even years after we enter adulthood and start our own families.

And yet, as marketers, we too often target a family based solely on who lives in a given household. Our family relationships are not bound by the walls of a home, or even by blood. They extend beyond income, social class, and geographic boundaries. To understand the real value of the New Heartland family we need to remind ourselves to:

- Look at familial relationships beyond traditional stereotypes and the confines of a home's four walls.

- Establish new metrics that take total extended family value into account, rather than just one individual family unit.

New Heartland residents are rather liberal in their definition of family, so it's important for brands to understand the big picture. What is considered extended family in other regions, to us, is just family. It expands well past the borders of the nuclear definition into multiple generations, in-laws, stepfamilies, and even those with no blood relationship at all.

To illustrate how broad our definition of family can be, consider how we define a cousin in the New Heartland. Few of us could ever limit ourselves to just the cousins produced by our parents' siblings. Rather, a cousin can be our first cousin, second cousin twice removed, cousin by marriage, step-cousin, the kids that grew up next door or the children of our best friend from high school. To us, they are all just family. Case in point: I'm Cousin Paul to the daughter of my wife's second cousin. I'm Uncle Paul to the daughter of a long-time, unrelated friend of the family. If we feel closer to you than friends, we'll make you family.

Beyond the ever-expanding, honorary family, the roles of the blood relatives are changing as well. The so-called 'nuclear family' is in the minority as, like the rest of the country, our family units are becoming more diverse.

MARKETING TO THE NON-NUCLEAR FAMILY

The families of today look a lot different than they did fifty years ago. With numbers rising for single-parent, multigenerational, and interracial households, there is no longer a standard snapshot of a typical American family. A Pew Research study found that one out of every ten U.S. children lives with a grandparent in the home.[30] They also reported a decline in young marriage with 20 percent of

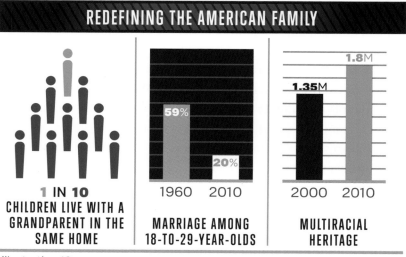

REDEFINING THE AMERICAN FAMILY

1 IN 10 CHILDREN LIVE WITH A GRANDPARENT IN THE SAME HOME

59% | 20%
1960 | 2010
MARRIAGE AMONG 18-TO-29-YEAR-OLDS

1.35M | 1.8M
2000 | 2010
MULTIRACIAL HERITAGE

Illustration 12

18-29-year-olds married in the latest census, compared to 59 percent in 1960.[31] The U.S. also saw a 133 percent increase, or nine million citizens, who claimed both black and white heritage since the previous Census.[32] The list goes on and on when we observe the transformation over the last few decades.

The changing face of American families might be great for our country's rich cultural diversity, but it can sure be a problem for marketers. How can we send targeted messaging without putting our audiences in those neat little categorized boxes?

If we're able to look past the surface of the outward appearance of families and get right to the essence of what's important to them, we'll see that regardless of their choices in how they form their household, they actually have a lot in common. In the New Heartland, regardless of age, gender, or race, from almost everyone I spoke with, it was the three pillars—Faith, Community, and Family—that I found to be the shared foundation upon which decisions were based. You'll find that focusing on these core values provides an excellent way to reach New Heartland families of all types.

Let's say you'd like to depict the changing face of the American family. In a recent Cheerios commercial, we saw just that. In the spot, a little girl approaches her mom and says, "Mom, Dad told me that Cheerios is good for your heart. Is that true?" The mom replies, "It says here that Cheerios has whole grain oats that can help remove some cholesterol and that's heart healthy." The girl takes the box and runs out of the room. In the next shot, we see the father waking up from a nap and finding Cheerios poured all over his shirt, on top of his heart. It's an adorable spot featuring a beautiful family—one that just happens to be interracial.

The commercial made a lot of people take notice. Though interracial marriages have been depicted plenty of times before on television, it's not often that a large brand chooses that route for a national commercial.

General Mills marketing vice president Camille Gibson said that they chose an interracial family because, "Ultimately we were trying to portray an American family, and there are lots of multicultural families in America today."

Of course, some of the more negative reactions made better headlines and a few media outlets labeled the spot as controversial. But with a "Like" rating of more than 95 percent on YouTube from more than five million views (astounding for any commercial), the response has been overwhelmingly supportive.

CASE STUDY

Procter & Gamble for the Win

In 2012, Procter & Gamble (P&G) hit gold with their continued "Thank You, Mom" campaign. As a sponsor of the Olympic Games, the company decided to focus not only on the athletes, but the people behind them—their moms.

Created by Wieden + Kennedy in Portland, the 2012 spot for the London Games titled "Best Job" featured four athletes from four different cities around the world. It follows their Olympic journey from small children to grown professionals. Their mothers are shown in the important, yet often overlooked role that is necessary in the success of these athletes, such as preparing meals, transporting them to practice, washing their clothes, and, of course, acting as their cheering section. The commercial was a huge hit, landing on 'best of' ad lists for the year, and it even scored them an Emmy. Executives estimated that campaign generated more than $500,000 in sales.

The campaign continued in 2014 for the Sochi Winter Olympics. A spot opens with four different families highlighting mothers as they help teach their toddling babies to walk through a series of falls. We follow the same families as the children grow up, each pursuing a different winter sport: figure skating, skiing, snowboarding, and hockey. Through the years, the children experience physical and emotional setbacks as they work to perfect their talents. Scraped knees, sore feet, and tears of disappointment are all tended to by their loving and ever-present mothers. The final scenes see our now-grown athletes competing in and dominating the Olympic Games. I dare you to try to keep a dry eye as they run over to share their moments of glory with their moms at the end of the spot. A message afterwards reads, "For teaching us that falling only makes us stronger, thank you, Mom."

P&G extended the family-brand platform to social platforms with a unique Facebook page, specifically for the Thank You, Mom campaign.

Today, it has more than eight hundred thousand Likes, and fans still interact with it daily. The brand team also created a mobile app that could create a unique thank-you message to send to your own mother.

This was a massive campaign, by a hugely talented agency, for one of the world's biggest companies, at an event that attracts viewers worldwide. The message here is what was so popular and the idea could be executed on any level, with any budget. The message of thanking the family that stood behind us as we claim the glory is one that resonates worldwide, but the impact on the New Heartland consumer is substantial in creating brand loyalty. I would wager that New Heartlanders who were touched by the campaign's message view P&G brands in a positive light. The importance of family is a powerful core value and a great filter for brands to measure campaign effectiveness. And Procter & Gamble scored big in the New Heartland, as well as around the world by recognizing that.

» The definition of family here extends beyond shared genes. Close friends and extended relatives are all considered to be part of the family unit.

» Family traditions involve brands. In the New Heartland, loyalty to a brand can be passed through multiple generations.

» Our families, like the rest of America, are a great blend of ages, races, and generations. The common threads that bind us together are our values.

Just like getting to know any new friend, you tend to connect over hobbies and interests. It's the same for the New Heartland. You've gotten to know who we are in Part One, now let's discuss where we are. In this section we'll cover my Five Channels of Access. These are the places where New Heartlanders hang out on the weekends, the activities that we share with our kids, and the passions that claim our disposable income.

These channels include Music, Food, Sports, Outdoors, and Social spaces. Understanding what makes the New Heartland unique in these areas is an important step in connecting with us. We'll cover brands that have had triumphs and missteps along the way to help you craft your brand strategy. We'll also cover how those all-important Core Values play into creating a successful New Heartland relationship.

PART TWO

FIVE WAYS TO REACH THE NEW HEARTLAND

CHAPTER

5 MUSIC

THE NEW HEARTLAND + MUSIC

| NEW HEARTLANDERS **33%** MORE LIKELY to prefer COUNTRY | NON-NEW HEARTLANDERS **60%** MORE LIKELY to prefer POP |

COUNTRY IS #1 FORMAT—AGES 18-54

43% of brand loyal adults are **COUNTRY FANS** (more than any other genre)

AND OF THOSE FANS

72% OWN A **HOME**

30% HAVE A HOUSEHOLD **INCOME OF $100K+**

64% ARE **MARRIED**

96% OWN A **MOBILE PHONE**

89% ARE ON **FACEBOOK**

58% ARE ON **TWITTER**

Cognitive neuroscience research has established that our choices are influenced by emotional reactions of which we may not be consciously aware. Malcolm Gladwell, in his bestseller, *Blink*, calls this "the power of thinking without thinking." How many times have you heard a song and been instantly transported to a time/place of your past?

Music is an enormously powerful medium, and it is wholly embraced in the New Heartland.

You can see the power music has with recall and association through popular movies or famous ads. Think about *Jaws* and the infamous track that begins to play as the shark gets near. Is it playing in your head right now? That ominous beat is one unlikely to be forgotten by those who experienced the terror and fear of open water that the movie instilled. The same can be said for many TV show theme songs such as *Good Times, Cheers, Friends, Happy Days, The Andy Griffith Show, Breaking Bad, Downton Abbey, Mad Men* ... the list goes on. The fact that we are still able to instantly recall the *Jaws* theme as well as old TV show theme songs many years after they aired, shows just how powerful audio branding can be.

Audio branding can be very beneficial in helping consumers connect with a product or company. The emotional response elicited from music is often associated with a product and aids in the development of a customer's feelings about a brand. This is why it's so important to ensure that the music or artist with which you align is representative of your business and beliefs. Your customers can appreciate supporting a company that partners with a brand ambassador whose values align with their own.

THE MUSIC THAT'S ROCKING SALES NATIONWIDE

If you're interested in connecting with the New Heartland through music, country music should be high on your consideration list.

Country music is dominating airwaves, ticket sales, merchandise sales, and album purchases in the New Heartland and nationwide. An astounding 102 million country music consumers are in the United States, 20 million live in the West, 14 million in the Northeast, and the rest live in ... you guessed it—the New Heartland.[33] Country music is, in fact, the No. 1-reported radio format for audiences spanning in age from 18 to 54, and the No. 2 format for 12- to 17-year-olds and consumers ages 55 and older.[34] New York actually comes in as the top location for country album sales. Album sales by percentage of population show that the top ten locations are all in the New Heartland.

The audience for the country music genre now parallels the U.S. consumer base, spanning the nation as well as cultural and socioeconomic brackets. Plus, country fans' annual household incomes now skew toward the higher end—averaging $75,000 in 2013—making them appealing for brands targeting higher-earning consumers.[35] And don't forget the loyalty factor ... country music fans are the most die-hard, loyal fans of any genre. As evidence, witness the phenomenon of the annual CMA Music Festival, which drew an estimated eighty thousand attendees this year. Here, fans are given the rare opportunity to get up close and personal with their favorite artist. From new to superstar acts, all of the artists participate in fan club activities to thank their fans for supporting their careers.

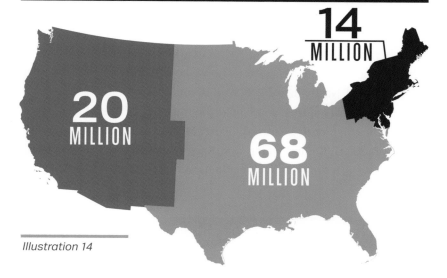

Illustration 14

The format has welcomed many new artists that have a big cross-over appeal, making it more accessible to a wider range of music fans. Many artists including Jason Aldean, Carrie Underwood, Tim McGraw, Lady Antebellum, Zac Brown, and Taylor Swift all find themselves popular among listeners of other genres. The remix of Florida Georgia Line's "Cruise," featuring Nelly, hit the airwaves on every pop and country radio station for months.

"Big name country stars are of the same status as pop music stars right now," says Kathy Gardner, global head of the DBI at RepuCom, an industry leader in sports marketing research. "They're relatable, and that's key. (Country stars) scored well in the most important factors that contribute to consumers making a purchase: trustworthiness, likability, and 'breakthrough,' meaning that when you see them on TV, you pay attention to what they are saying."[36]

Country music is showing its impact on television as well. The 2013 CMA Awards drew more than 16 million viewers, demonstrating that

America is tuning in to the tube as well as the radio.[37] The influence on network programming is easy to see as well. *Nashville*, a show (nighttime soap opera) about the lives of fictional country music artists, posted strong viewer numbers in its first two seasons. The numbers were so strong that the network renewed the show for a third season. The success of the show also drove significant interest to the city of Nashville as well. And if you take a look at the history of *American Idol* alums, you'll hear the majority of them belting out their tunes on country stations: Scotty McCreery, Carrie Underwood, Kelly Clarkson, Kellie Pickler, and Kree Harrison. Twelve of *American Idol*'s thirteen winners over the years have come from the New Heartland.[38]

AMERICAN IDOL WINNERS FROM THE NEW HEARTLAND

1 Kelly Clarkson
Burleson, TX

2 Ruben Studdard
Birmingham, AL

3 Fantasia Barrino
High Point, NC

4 Carrie Underwood
Checotah, OK

5 Taylor Hicks
Birmingham, AL

6 Jordin Sparks
Glendale, AZ

7 David Cook
Blue Springs, MO

8 Kris Allen
Conway, AK

9 Lee DeWyze
Mount Prospect, IL

10 Scotty McCreery
Garner, NC

11 Phillip Phillips
Leesburg, GA

12 Candice Glover
St. Helena Island, SC

13 Caleb Johnson
Asheville, NC

Illustration 15

● New Heartland

"The stereotypes about the country music listener are that they're rural, they're downscale, and they're not very tech-savvy, but our research shows that that's all bunk," says Chris Ackerman, vice president of Coleman Insights, a media research firm. "The country music audience is largely suburban, a mix of white- and blue-collar, and a lot more affluent than even the country industry itself thought. They're a much more attractive target for marketers than might have been perceived."

An interesting aspect of country music is how it's able to appeal to such a wide demographic. In no other format will you see such big numbers shared by both Millennials and Boomers. It's a common ground that's rare to find in any industry.

The success of the genre is not lost on the rest on the music industry. *Rolling Stone* recently opened an office in Nashville to run a stand-alone, country music-themed website. The most iconic music publication (maybe ever) understands the need to give country the platform it deserves. With a 4 percent increase in country album sales compared to a 2 percent increase in rock album sales, and an even more disappointing decrease in sales for alternative and R&B, it makes sense for the entire music industry to pay attention.[39]

TOP FIVE FAVORITE ARTISTS

NEW HEARTLAND	VS	NON-NEW HEARTLAND
1 The Beatles		1 The Beatles
2 Eagles		2 Taylor Swift
3 Luke Bryan		3 The Rolling Stones
4 The Rolling Stones		4 Katy Perry
5 George Strait		5 Bruce Springsteen

Illustration 16

COUNTRY ARTISTS CONNECT WITH CORE VALUES

Perhaps because of its crossover appeal, more listeners are able to find something they already like and recognize in country. I believe it also has to do with fans being able to more personally identify with the artists that makes it so approachable. It offers more "regular Joe" personalities than any other genre. Oftentimes, musicians throw on a ball cap and blue jeans to sing about daily life's joys and sorrows. It's easier for the general public to see themselves in an artist like this than a pop star like Lady Gaga, Justin Bieber, or Miley Cyrus, for example.

We see this in politics all of the time. Voters tend to connect with candidates that seem down-to-earth and relatable. So every election season, the suits are put away, the sleeves are rolled up, and the candidates get down to the business of being just like you. And this strategy does pay off on election day. Or in Mitt Romney's case, it didn't pay off because of the lack of an authentic connection.

Country musicians largely have a relatable personality, so the genre as a whole feels approachable and friendly. These perceived shared values that help fans feel connected goes back to the three core values of the New Heartland.

It's about Faith

Country stars are not afraid to acknowledge and celebrate their faith. This is very appealing to the New Heartland consumer who is starting to feel edged out of mainstream popular culture.

Megastars have put out hugely successful songs that openly discuss their faith. Carrie Underwood's "Jesus Take the Wheel" talks about a young single mother giving up control of her life to God. Brad Paisley's "When I Get Where I'm Going" is a heartfelt look at heaven. George Strait reflects on the many ways he can see God's work in "I Saw God Today," and Kenny Chesney sings about being saved in "Never Wanted Nothing More." Each of these songs, and many others that openly discuss faith, went to number one on the country charts.

It's about Family

Country stars are also famous for singing about the role their family has played in their life, both the family at home and also their extended family.

Turn on a country station and you won't have to wait long to hear a song written about or offering advice to a child, explaining how Mom or Dad shaped an artist's life, or about lessons Grandpa taught them. One of my favorites is Dierks Bentley's number-one song, "I Hold On."

It's about Community

Fans also love songs that extol the virtues of a close-knit, small-town community.

Songs like Eric Church's "Give Me Back My Hometown," Montgomery Gentry's "My Town," Craig Morgan's "That's What I Love about Sundays," Brooks and Dunn's "Red Dirt Road," and Alan Jackson's "Small Town Southern Man" cleverly mix pride in their hometown with faith and family. It's a powerful recipe.

If you want to understand the New Heartland lifestyle, look up the lyrics to any of these songs. That's who we are and that's how we feel about our hometown community, family, and faith.

This sort of connection with a music hero can yield powerful results for brands that support them as well. Country consumers post some impressive numbers concerning brand loyalty.

Be careful not to stereotype, because not every country act is about drinking sweet tea on the front porch after Sunday church. If your brand needs an edge, check out performers like Eric Church, Brantley Gilbert, and The Cadillac Three. There's a country act for almost every brand.

Pepsi's Iconic Summer with Blake Shelton

Pepsi-Cola was created in a drug store in New Berlin, North Carolina, in 1898. In 1909, the brand partnered with its first celebrity, pioneer car racer Barney Oldfield. The brand has gone on to represent "What's Now" in pop culture through its many partnerships with some of the world's top athletes and celebrities.

Pepsi continued the tradition as they prepared to roll out their 2013 "Iconic Summer" platform. The campaign celebrated cultural icons by offering consumers fun summer rewards and impossible-to-buy access to great music and events. Finding that right celebrity partnership to bring the platform to life and leverage their Country Music Association (CMA) Music Fest sponsorship was key.

Blake Shelton was the perfect fit. His professional success with twelve consecutive number-one hits, multiple music awards and status as an outspoken and lovable judge on the hit TV show "The Voice" justifies his superstar status. But his values, transparency, and easygoing personality have helped him connect with New Heartland fans for years.

"The cool thing about country artists and country fans is the connection that we have. I don't look at them as fans, I look at them as buddies, and we're all hanging out together in a concert situation," Shelton told *Billboard* at the top of CMA Week. "Pepsi wants music fans to have a chance to have a summer they won't forget, and that's how I felt about this summer going out on my first really big headlining tour. That's something I won't forget. They're also giving away tons of prizes, and I even saw somebody in there is gonna win a trip to the Super Bowl. You think I won't be trying to enter that one? I'll be putting my name in for that one."[40]

In addition to Shelton, who made appearances for Iconic Summer throughout the summer, Pepsi supported the program through its sponsorships of Beyoncé's The Mrs. Carter Show World Tour, the MLB All Star Game, the MTV Video Music Awards, the iHeartRadio Music Festival, and

the Pepsi Gulf Coast Jam. For each event, Pepsi fans had a chance to win exclusive tickets and meet-and-greets by uploading photos and participating in other fan engagements.

One of the significant ways Pepsi leveraged Blake Shelton for the Iconic Summer kickoff was a two-minute video displayed on Pepsi.com, Pepsi's official YouTube channel and all PepsiCo digital platforms. The video of Shelton was recorded to enhance Pepsi.com as an interactive, multimedia music platform that features engaging content to drive repeat visits from fans.

The most exciting piece of Shelton's integration with the campaign kickoff was his appearance at the CMA Music Festival. Pepsi's goal was to walk away with a short, shareable video that leveraged the festival sponsorship and Shelton's surprise appearance to create the ultimate fan experience.

Fans gathered at the Pepsi tent and entered into a drawing for the opportunity to compete in a Pepsi Speed Sketch event to win tickets to Shelton's performance that evening. He surprised fans by showing up to compete with them. The end result was a two-minute video that conveys the fun and excitement, producing a perfect "Iconic" moment, and kickoff to an "Iconic Summer." The video generated hundreds of thousands of views via Pepsi digital channels.

Blake Shelton provided the brand with national notoriety coupled with a deeply rooted connection to the New Heartland consumer.

The result was a seamless promotion and a mutually beneficial partnership that resonated with Pepsi's consumers, and led to an even more robust brand partnership with Blake in 2014.

» Utilizing the right music in campaigns increases brand recall and likelihood of purchase.

» The emotional response elicited from music can be transferred to the product or company that uses it.

» The country genre attracts the widest age demographic as the number-one-reported format for the 25-54-year-old set, and number two for the 18-24-year-old crowd.

» Country music and artists have a tremendous crossover appeal, with both enjoying regular air time on pop and rock stations, thereby reaching an even larger fan base.

» Don't forget to factor in the cost of licensing music for your campaigns. In most cases artists cannot give brand partners the use of their music. This requires an expert to negotiate a fair rate and use for the music.

KEY POINTS: MUSIC

CHAPTER

6 FOOD

THE NEW HEARTLAND + FOOD

NEW HEARTLAND WOMEN ARE **62%** MORE LIKELY TO **PREFER** COMFORT FOOD OVER GOURMET FOOD

NEW HEARTLANDERS
44% more likely to be a "BEER AND BOURBON" CROWD

NEW HEARTLAND ●
NON-NEW HEARTLAND ●

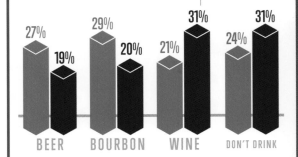

	BEER	BOURBON	WINE	DON'T DRINK
New Heartland	27%	29%	21%	24%
Non-New Heartland	19%	20%	31%	31%

80% OF THE NATION'S BARBECUE FESTIVALS AND COMPETITIONS ARE IN THE NEW HEARTLAND

NEW HEARTLAND **19%** MORE LIKELY — TO SAY — **FOOD**

WHAT IS BBQ?

NON-NEW HEARTLAND **21%** MORE LIKELY — TO SAY — **EVENT**

Illustration 17

Food is far more than just sustenance in the New Heartland—it's a social experience. Whether it's the actual preparation of the food or gathering to enjoy the end product, food is an important link to our culture, a source of identity, and an excuse to gather with family and friends. Understanding the role food plays in our lifestyle is important, because it provides a unique opportunity for brands to reach us in a tasteful way.

Our love of food is legendary. According to our New Heartland Consumer Insights Study (and probably not a surprise to anyone), comfort food is the fare of choice over gourmet food in the New Heartland, compared to the non-New Heartland by an 8:1 ratio. However, the non-New Heartland loves it, too![41]

To understand our current culinary tastes, however, you must first understand our history. Many of our famous dishes were created by the innovation of poor farmers just trying to feed their families. A couple hundred years ago in the rural New Heartland, people had to be very resourceful just to stay alive. There were few cities, no grocery stores, and cheap transportation into town to buy food was unheard of. Food was often scarce, so they had to make do with what was available, and they wasted nothing.

Poor farmers were limited to scant rations of cornmeal and pork, along with whatever they could grow or hunt. Their resourcefulness and creativity evolved into a new form of southern cuisine, which is the foundation of today's southern soul food.

With little access to meat itself, poor farmers would use every last bit of the animal that was edible. The fatty skin of a pig became pork rinds, which are still available in groceries and truck stops all over the New Heartland. The organs became sweetbreads, chitlins (pig intestines), and hog maw (pig stomach). Leftover vegetable cuttings, called bitter greens, were sautéed with pork fat or bacon drippings, and collard greens were invented. This is still served all over the South (although that doesn't mean I eat it). Biscuits and gravy, grits, and chicken fried steak are also food staples here and another example of innovation with simple, accessible ingredients.

The Midwest developed its own regional dishes as well. It's cattle country here, so expect some tasty, oversized steaks. Also known as "America's Breadbasket," the farmland is rich with crops such as wheat, corn, and a myriad vegetables. A million different versions of casseroles exist today because of the wives that created a smart way to feed families with what was available to them.

But the thing that's most indicative of New Heartland culinary culture is the social component. We will use any excuse to fire up the grill and break out the baking pans to get friends or family together. It's not a proper gathering unless food is involved. It's also how we share our congratulations, condolences, and celebrations. Food is a key component of our lifestyle and woven into our core values.

If you get sick or lose a loved one, you can almost be assured you have covered dishes coming your way from people eager to help lessen the stress load. On Sunday afternoon, you'll find churches around the New Heartland filled with members, bonding over a meal. We bake cakes for fundraising, tailgate before a game, and hold entire events around cooking a special food item. Have you ever been to a crawfish boil? I highly recommend you get invited to one soon. The list of specialty food items goes on and on, but we'll concentrate on a few key items that demonstrate just how important food is to the New Heartland culture.

WHAT'S FOR DINNER?

I've heard it said that the most-treasured recipes in the New Heartland originally came off the label of a Campbell's soup can, Cool Whip container, or a Jell-O carton. I realize many readers didn't even know there were recipes on the back of these labels; if you did, you couldn't imagine who in their right mind would ever use them. But for some reason, people here love them. Purely out of convenience, the basic principle is that most of the ingredients come out of a can or box.

Casseroles can also have these traits. This is one of the dishes that you're likely to see in some form at every gathering. Everybody has his or her own special recipes. It can be a dessert, side item, main dish, or starter. Just about any ingredient you can think of has probably found its way into a casserole at some point. I think it's more about the gesture than it is the quality of the dish, but surprisingly most of the casseroles taste great.

Casseroles are a mix of food items prepared and served in a dish. Some popular ones here are green bean, sweet potato, baked chicken, or mac & cheese varieties. We also like concoctions mixing cream-of-anything soup and tuna or chicken, usually with rice or some type of pasta. Think high-carb, high-calorie, comfort food.

These dishes are usually easy to make, are filling and can be easily transported. The practicality of the casserole definitely helps make it so popular.

Lightening the load was the impetus behind the brilliant creation of MealTrain.com. According to their site, Meal Train co-founder Kathleen Laramee volunteered to organize the giving of meals, known as a meal train, to support a neighborhood family after the birth of a new baby.

As the organizer, Kathleen made a list of the family's meal preferences and preferred dates in addition to collecting names of friends and neighborhood parents who had expressed interest in participating in the meal train. Once the baby arrived, she sent an e-mail to each family asking them to contact her to book a night.

While enjoying her role, Kathleen was frequently asked the same questions from the potential givers: "What days are they available?" "What do they like to eat?" "What have they already had?" "What don't they like?" "Are there any allergies?" "How many should I cook for?" "Can I reschedule?" In addition, the recipient family was also asking questions: "Who is delivering tonight?" "Can we invite more people?" "Can you tell people not to bring any more soup?"

MealTrain.com is a free solution that simplifies the organization of giving and receiving meals. By allowing the giving party to take into account the recipient's preferred meal times, food preferences, and available days, the site helps ensure that the recipient gets the meals they enjoy on the days that are most helpful. Necessity truly is the mother of invention!

BARBECUE: A NOUN OR VERB?

Barbecue is another top food in the New Heartland. Here, it's a noun, not a verb. My friends on the coasts like to barbecue, which means they grill out. And what they grill isn't important; rather, the act of grilling itself is "barbecue" to them. For them, it's a verb, something one does, not something one eats.

However, in the New Heartland, barbecue is slow-smoked beef, ribs (beef, pork, and turkey), pork, turkey, and even kielbasa. We don't barbecue—we eat barbecue.

This delicacy is very important to the New Heartland culture, and we take it very seriously. According to BBQ-festivals.com, there are 138 barbecue festivals and competitions around the country each year, 80 percent of which are held in the New Heartland. I can't help but think the other 20 percent were created by BBQ fans transplanted from the New Heartland, who find themselves homesick and miss their favorite smoked meat and sides.

Memphis is home to the best 'Q' in the civilized world, in my opinion. They celebrate the pig at the Memphis in May World Championship Barbecue Contest. Held on a bluff overlooking the mighty Mississippi River in downtown Memphis, the contest draws hundreds of teams that compete for more than $100,000 in prizes and worldwide bragging rights.

While meat smoking is the main theme, the contest wouldn't be complete without the Mr. Piggy Idol comparison, which involves grown men in tutus and snouts and women kicking their heels (hooves) up. Cold beer, live music, and the best barbecue you'll ever eat, makes this festival a must-add to your bucket list.

Barbecue varies greatly, depending on where you are in the New Heartland. In Kentucky its pulled mutton, and in Texas it's sliced beef brisket. No matter where you are, it's all smoked.

In most other barbecue states, it's pork. North Carolina serves it in a peppery vinegar sauce, while South Carolina and Georgia serve it in a sauce created using yellow mustard. In Memphis, they pull the pork and soak it in a sweet tomato-based sauce with pepper and molasses, or serve ribs in a similar sauce or dry rub. In Alabama, they offer pulled and chopped pork as well as ribs in a spicier tomato-based sauce.

Regardless of the ingredients and method of preparation, one thing all New Heartland chefs will agree on is that it takes time. Barbecue, whether pulled pork, sliced brisket, or smoked ribs, is cooked "low and slow" to get that fall-off-the-bone texture.

I personally think barbecue is so popular because preparing food is an occasion, so when we're not casseroling, we love things that take a really long time to make. Friends and family typically will join forces to make barbecue, which gives them an excuse to sit around and shoot the bull, so-to-speak, for several hours. It's a social event. And the end result is well worth the wait.

Barbecue and casseroles, though very different, both heavily promote the idea of community. Their very purpose often involves bringing people together. Whether for a church event, or a small family gathering, our special foods help us bond and strengthen relationships. It's more than just ingredients—these rituals reinforce our important cultural traditions.

JustAPinch.com Creates Online Community of Food Lovers

JustAPinch.com is one of the fastest-growing and engaged digital platforms for food lovers across the New Heartland. This online platform was launched by American Hometown Media, the same founders that created the publishing group behind the successful *American Profile* magazine insert delivered to American households through local community newspapers. The JustAPinch.com website inspiration was created in response to the popularity and demand of the user-submitted recipes section of the newspaper insert.

American Hometown Media listened and learned from their core audience, and they discovered some interesting things about what their readers really wanted. Most food blogs and cooking shows showcase gourmet recipes with complicated ingredients that appeal to chefs. But in reality, most women who cook for the family don't have the time or want to spend the money on making those types of recipes.

Dan Hammond, president and chief executive officer of American Hometown Media, explains: "They all aspire to cook these chef-inspired dishes, but in an interesting phenomenon, an overwhelming majority of these women wake up from that dream and find themselves pushing a shopping cart down the grocery aisle and buying boxed pasta and canned spaghetti sauce. They're not hand-cranking out pasta at home, and they're not buying fresh arugula."

The company also made another key observation that changed the way they delivered their brand messaging. They found that with food and recipes, non-professional photography was much more effective than professional photos. Women who saw a slightly grainy picture of a dish on a regular dinner plate in an everyday kitchen, experienced an instant connection—she would know instinctually that she could cook that because someone else had cooked that dish in their home kitchen. And

a photograph of the woman who had submitted her recipe, her bio, and her personal comments about the dish established trust, and a sense of shared interests.

These observations formed the foundation of JustAPinch.com, a place where everyday moms and cooks virtually congregate to share recipes, trade cooking tips, and soak up the recognition they deserve for their creations. They have tapped into a common core value of community, while leveraging two key lifestyle channels for reaching and engaging the New Heartlander: Food and Digital/Social engagement.

The results speak for themselves. In the first three years, the website has become the largest repository of user-posted recipes in the world, boasting an astounding 350,000+ community-submitted dishes to date. The company ended 2013 with 1 million registered users and 10 million unique visitors, and predicted that by the end of 2014, they will have 2 million registered users and 20 million unique visitors.

Engagement levels on the website boast an average of sixteen minutes per session, one to three times a day, indicating that these visitors love to hang out on the site. American Hometown Media has created a successful brand with JustAPinch.com with a loyal following who are spreading the word like wildfire. The site has become far more than a place to get ideas for dinner; it also is a very active social network in its own right. More than 230,000 fans on Facebook and 30,000 followers on Pinterest keep the cooking tips coming daily, and the word-of-mouth advertising spreading.

JustAPinch.com is wildly popular in the New Heartland. It's popularity is based on the strong ties to community and cultural relevancy. Their success lies in the fact that they created online what exists in the real world—an active and engaged community of parents, grandparents, old pros, and beginners, swapping recipes and sharing experiences. Their discovery about members preferring real food photos from other home cooks speaks to the very essence of the New Heartland consumer. They want messaging that speaks about things that matter to them in a way they can personally relate to.

JustAPinch.com is a great example of a multi-dimensional and integrated brand platform that satisfies the needs and desires of a very active and fiercely brand loyal group of New Heartland consumers.

Real Recipes from
Real Home Cooks

» Food is an expression of our culture.

» The preparation can be just as communal as enjoying it. It's a way we spend time with our families and communities.

» Like most of the world, our regional cuisine is greatly influenced by our history and geography. The rural landscape and economic challenges of our past resulted in the creation of simple recipes from readily available ingredients.

» Barbecue is something we eat, not something we do in the New Heartland.

CHAPTER

7

SPORTS

THE NEW HEARTLAND + SPORTS

NEW HEARTLANDERS ARE MORE THAN **TWICE AS LIKELY** TO PREFER COLLEGE SPORTS

····· HOME TO ·····

9 OF THE **TOP 10** SPORTS REVENUE-GENERATING COLLEGES

── AND ──

18 OF THE **20** MOST LOYAL FAN STATES

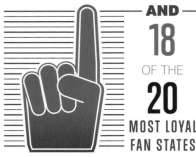

YOUTH U.S. SPORTS

$7 BILLION
INDUSTRY

8 OF 10 BEST STATES FOR HIGH SCHOOL FOOTBALL ARE IN THE NEW HEARTLAND

44% MORE LIKELY TO BE INVOLVED IN HIGH SCHOOL/YOUTH SPORTS

NASCAR is the **#1 spectator sport** in the U.S.

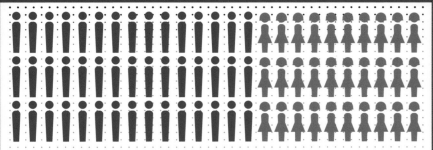

75 MILLION NASCAR FANS ▸ 40% ARE WOMEN

ONE FIFTH of **FORTUNE 500 COMPANIES** SPONSOR NASCAR

Fans are **63%** more likely to consider a brand that is an official sponsor of **NASCAR**

Illustration 18

Brand marketers have partnered with sports teams, events, and individual athletes to grab consumers' attention for more than a century, whether that's sponsoring the local Little League team, displaying superstar athletes on a cereal box, or dropping more than $133,000 per second on Super Bowl ads.[42]

But as costs have skyrocketed over the years, brands have turned a more critical eye on their sports marketing expenditures to examine if the return on investment includes more than just box seats and an autographed ball for the CEO.

In the New Heartland, sports can be a particularly effective and even cost-effective tool for reaching the consumer, as long as it's the right sport.

Like any other red-blooded American, we in the New Heartland love our sports. We spend summers at the ball field, follow the drama on the court, and will put our fantasy league teams up against anybody's, any day. But there are a few sectors that seem to be just a little more prevalent in the New Heartland than in other parts of the country—college sports, any kind of car or truck racing, and hometown youth sports.

Although three very separate activities, these sectors share one key component—fanatic loyalty. This devotion is seen in the support New Heartland fans show for the athletes, teams, communities, and the brands who sponsor them. We always post big numbers, not only in attendance and TV viewership, but also in merchandise sales and online engagement.

COLLEGE SPORTS PERSONIFY NEW HEARTLAND CORE VALUES

If you ask a New Heartland resident about their favorite team, chances are they'll name a *college* football or basketball team, as revealed in our New Heartland Consumer Insights Study. The pros are huge, too. But college sports are the personification of the New Heartland's core values.

Here, your old alma mater is more than just an institution for academic excellence; it's also the determining factor for how you will spend the majority of your Saturdays from spring football to bowl games. Supporting your college team is a seriously big deal here.

In simple numbers, you can quickly see our big support. Of the twenty biggest football stadiums in the U.S., the New Heartland claims fifteen, with fourteen of those being college stadiums. There are so many fans, we have to go bigger than the pros! *Bleacher Report* recently ranked fan loyalty across the 125 Football Bowl Subdivision teams and declared eighteen of the top twenty to be from New Heartland states.[43] The Southeastern Conference (SEC) has dominated the Bowl Championship Series, having won seven consecutive titles through the 2012 season, making it the most dominant football conference in the country. This domination fuels a nearly maniacal love for college sports.

The NCAA shows our near unbelievable support of college football in the New Heartland with their recently released report outlining fan attendance.[44] Michigan led the list with an astounding average of 111,592 fans at their home games in 2013. They were followed by

Ohio State with 104,933, then Alabama with 101,505. The SEC as a whole enjoyed its sixteenth consecutive year as reigning champ in the category, averaging 75,674 per game.

Our New Heartland Consumer Insights Study backs up this difference with more than twice as many New Heartlanders claiming to prefer college sports.[45]

Illustration 19

In my case, I was raised on Notre Dame. With parents being native to South Bend, Indiana, home of the Fighting Irish, it's all they knew, even though they didn't attend the University themselves. But that's actually common: many of the biggest college sports fans I have come across did not attend the school they support. I have many relatives in South Bend who could be the poster children for New Heartland values: they work hard, play harder, and love the Irish. So what if Notre Dame isn't their alma mater? They are loyal, and that's a New Heartland value.

Most of the time, these uber-fans come from families that have been fans of the same team for generations. Some New Heartland residents might even admit to purposefully brainwashing their young kids into being fans before, heaven forbid, they start cheering for a rival. For example, my wife's father graduated from and played football for Vanderbilt University. She graduated from the University of Tennessee. A house divided.

Being from Memphis, I didn't have as strong of a connection with Notre Dame as my parents and cousins had. I grew up in UT country (University of Tennessee-Knoxville not UT Texas) and the Vols dominated the conversation across the state. Once I graduated from UT, my connection was cemented. As a twenty-six-year football season ticket holder, I've hung with the team through good, bad, and very bad times (Derek Dooley, Lane Kiffin), and I'll even don a muted version of the obnoxious UT orange for a game. My daughter and son both attend UT, and odds are, my other two kids will heavily consider it. Although I encouraged them to look outside the South for their undergrad, the value of the education was hard to pass up; thus, the next generation of a UT fan is born.

One of the biggest, most-storied rivalries is played out every November via the "Iron Bowl." Alabama and Auburn play this always heated game the Saturday after Thanksgiving. The 2013 game, played in Auburn, came down to a last-second field goal attempt by Bama. The kick was short and returned by Auburn 109 yards for the game-winning touchdown. After church the next day, I asked a diehard Alabama fan if they went to the game. Appalled at the question (and reeling from the fresh loss) she disgustingly said, "We would never set foot in Auburn!" Now that's deep-rooted fandom.

Ties to our favorite college team are lifelong, and fans aren't afraid to show their support through their time and wallet. *Business Insider* ranks nine out of the top ten universities that generated the most revenue for the 2013 football season as being from the New Heartland.[46] We travel to games home and away, dressing ourselves and our kids in the school colors. According to the *Sports Business Journal*, college fans support sponsors of their favorite teams more than their MLB and NBA fan counterparts. Only the NFL counts more avid fans (85 million) than avid fans of college sports (64 million).[47]

The games aren't always a single-day event. RVs start to set up around the stadium days before the game as loyal ticket holders make the

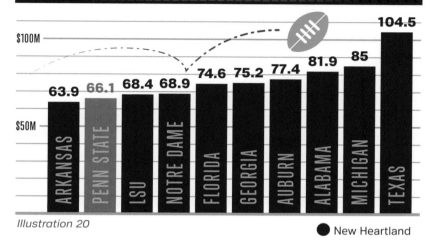

2013 HIGHEST UNIVERSITY REVENUES FROM FOOTBALL

Illustration 20

⬤ New Heartland

event a multi-day affair. If you happen to be around a big SEC school near football game day, take a drive through campus and see how many early birds you can find already firing up the grill outside their RVs or behind their SUVs.

SO, WHAT'S THE BIG DEAL WITH THE NEW HEARTLAND AND COLLEGE FOOTBALL?

Community—This core value plays a big role in our love for college sports. As you know by now, we tend to stick around our hometowns and home states. The shared love for the big schools is something we have in common with our community as the likelihood of our neighbors supporting the same school is much greater. It provides a camaraderie we feel even before stepping on campus. So a game symbolizes much more than just an athletic contest—it's about our personal identity and hometown pride.

Family—We love to pass things along to the next generation, and that includes our love for a team. If you grew up in the New Heartland

with a parent who supported a college team, chances are you were a fan before you could read. You've been to the games, taken the tour through campus and down memory lane. And the odds are that you choose the same school to continue your education. We're proud of our family traditions and it shows even in sports.

Geography—The New Heartland states give us a little more room to spread out. It also means we have a lower population density. If you look at New York City for example, you'll find twenty-two Division I schools. In Iowa, they have only two that play football, creating a much smaller chance for divided loyalties.

NASCAR BOASTS NEW HEARTLAND FANATICS

If you want to see some serious numbers and admirable brand loyalty, look no further than NASCAR. This is a sport that we, and much of the world, are simply crazy about. The colorful past of this sport is something of legends, but is absolutely true. Originally used as a way for moonshiners to evade the law, the original stock racing cars ran the drink by night and raced each other by day. Pastures were carved out to create the first racetracks, where locals would gather on weekends to watch races between cars reaching an astounding 120 miles per hour in the 1930s. As the sport grew in popularity, so did the need for formalized competition. The National Association for Stock Car Auto Racing (or NASCAR) was formed in 1948. The average attendance for an event is just under 100,000.[48] That's the average! Only a small handful of football stadiums in the U.S. even have enough seats to accommodate such a large crowd.

The sport posts some big numbers, but probably the biggest draw for a marketer is the brand loyalty these fans show. According to a recent *Turnkey Sports & Entertainment* study, NASCAR fans are 63 percent more likely to consider a brand that is an official sponsor of the sport. And a study from NASCAR and *Sports Illustrated* found that 66 percent of fans were willing to pay more for a sponsor's product.[54] Furthermore, an amazing finding was that 36 percent of NASCAR fans could name every sponsor of the top thirty ranked cars. Now, that's incredible news for brands.[55]

The stats look great, but there are still some things you'll need to know before jumping in. To see a high level of success, get your wallet ready because results like these don't come cheap and easy. First, you have to understand what NASCAR is really all about. You must experience several races firsthand. The stats don't capture the unique culture surrounding these events. Sure, their viewing numbers are strong, but the place where fans really connect with brands is at the track.

There is a lot of activity surrounding the races. It's a multiday affair for many racegoers. Fans get to walk through the garages to see the cars, take part in the many sponsored events, and even meet their favorite drivers. Racing is one of the few sports where fans can interact with the athletes on a personal level. There are also often multiple races to enjoy over the course of a weekend. It's this level of interaction that makes the races such an immersive and enjoyable experience for dedicated fans.

HERE ARE A FEW QUICK STATS:

- *NASCAR is the number-one spectator sport in the U.S.*
- *The three largest racing series sanctioned by NASCAR as of 2014 are the Sprint Cup Series, the Nationwide Series, and the Camping World Truck Series.[49]*
- *More than one-fifth of the Fortune 500 companies are currently NASCAR sponsors,[50] more than any other sport.[51]*
- *There are 75 million fans, 40 percent of which are women.[52]*
- *Daytona International Speedway saw 15 percent of U.S. adults last year, while an additional 18 percent watched a NASCAR event at home.[53]*

Second, prominently sponsoring a driver/team will set you back many millions. It takes quite a bit of money to keep the drivers on the track. The crew, car, training, gas, and travel quickly burn through the budget. Sponsorship dollars are vital to the growth of the sport. Thankfully, fans understand this, and as a result they enthusiastically support their driver's sponsors.

With big money investments, sponsors expect big returns—even from within the NASCAR organization. A program called NASCAR Fuel for Business was created to give sponsors an opportunity to buy and sell products to each other at discounted prices as well as make sponsorship deals inside and outside of the sport. NASCAR chief sales officer, Jim O'Connell, reported that through the program, Ford generated more than $200 million in vehicle sales in one year.[56]

YOUTH SPORTS PLAY UP FAMILY AND COMMUNITY TIME

Another sports experience that we're big fans of here doesn't actually have a lot to do with the sport itself, but the players in the game instead.

Youth sports takes a big part of family time for many New Heartlanders. Like the rest of the country, we wake up early to take the kids to their Saturday Little League games or load up the car for another weekend of travel ball. We start them ridiculously young; my kids started playing soccer at four years old.

At least where we live, gone are the days of playing multiple sports for your school. Youth sports have become so competitive that by the time they get to high school, kids have already specialized in one primary

sport. The demanding travel ball schedule has forced many young athletes into a near year-round commitment to their sport ... just to stay competitive. It's crazy the amount of time and money we dedicate to giving our kids the opportunity to earn a spot on their school or travel team. Many times, commitments to multiple teams might become too demanding to continue to pursue alongside academics and clubs. Athletes also find the level of competition is heightened dramatically at this stage since a select few elite athletes have the possibility of earning a college scholarship.

Today's world of athletics for the young is vastly different from what we knew it to be as kids. Special camps, private coaches, and tournaments beckon kids to "reach their potential." Parents can/do spend thousands of dollars to make sure that their children are trained by the very best coaches. Dance competitions draw thousands to travel across multiple state lines to perform their routines. Even big corporations have something to offer aspiring athletes. World-class brands, such as Nike and Adidas, offer elite programs for top performers in soccer, basketball, football, and other sports.

The MaxPreps Freeman Rankings is an objective system that determines the hierarchy for high school sports teams based on team victories, quality wins, and strength of schedule. Using these rankings, we can see just how big football is in the New Heartland. Eight of the top ten states for the best high school football are in the New Heartland.[57] These aren't specific schools; these are the averages for the entire state, which is very telling of the penetration of sports into our culture. For parents and players in-the-know that are serious about higher-level playing, sometimes a move to a better-known high school can get an athlete attention from college scouts.

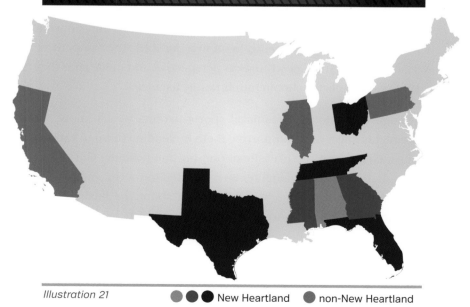

TOP 10 HIGH SCHOOL FOOTBALL STATES

Illustration 21

⬤ ⬤ ⬤ New Heartland   ⬤ non-New Heartland

All of this amounts to a huge economic impact. Youth sports have blown up in recent years to become a $7 billion industry.[58] Parents are forking out for uniforms, program fees, camps, and travel expenses. Brands can be a big help to financially stretched parents not only by sponsorships, but also scholarship awards or special discounts for traveling teams. It's a win for brands that want to promote a healthy lifestyle and make a big impact in a local community at the same time.

Just why we spend so much time and money on our childrens' recreational activities varies from family to family. It might be something as aspirational as a college scholarship, or something as simple as support for our kids' interests. Or some loser parents try to make their kid the athlete they weren't, which leads to some great drama among the other parents. Regardless of the reason, it's a big part of family here and a perfect way for the right brands to begin a relationship.

Like many other parents, we supported our kids' sports aspirations. They all played soccer and basketball; my son also played baseball, football, and lacrosse. As they got older, they had to choose what sport they wanted to concentrate on in a quest to stay competitive. We always strived to keep things in perspective and made sure they maintained a sports/school/church/family balance.

Although we're not the maniacal sports parents we all know, we were highly engaged in supporting them by sending them to various camps, clinics and the occasional one-on-one training. Out of our four kids, the youngest daughter is committed to soccer, and playing travel and school ball. I learned the most about the business surrounding high school sports through my sons' high school football careers. It's amazing how many cottage businesses that attempt to extract money from parents by promising to provide their kids with college recruiting and training services.

I knew my son wasn't another Peyton Manning, so we never went very far down that path. (Brag alert) As the top quarterback in the district, he set several school records at his 6-A (2,000+ students) school but at barely five-foot-eleven and without Johnny Manziel's speed, he wasn't going to be able to play Division I football. He decided he didn't want to dedicate the time it took to be a college athlete at the Division II-III level, so after fourteen years of practices, games, injuries, celebrations, and tears, his career came to an end upon graduation this year. I know several dads who spent more than $3,000 on these so-called recruiting services and training camps with the hope of their son playing college ball. This is a numbers business, preying on emotional dads whose personal aspirations never came to fruition; these scams are a cash-suck. A good friend was in agony after he invested thousands of dollars prior to his son's senior year in high school only to watch as his boy barely made it onto the field. His dreams of a college football career were crushed.

This is the downside to the passion for sports in the New Heartland. That passion blinds many of us to the reality of playing sports beyond the high school level. However, this is the same passion that fuels our love for our sports teams and makes sports such an important connecting point for brands wanting to know us.

NASCAR Finds Success with Family Loyalty

NASCAR knows its fans. The races, while a party for some, serve as a family outing for most. The loyalty to the drivers and the sport in general is passed down through generations. The same often applies to the drivers themselves. Bobby and Davey Allison, Lee and Richard Petty, and Dale Earnhardt Sr. and Jr. are just a few of the legendary father/son drivers that fans have been cheering on for decades.

In a very creative ad campaign, NASCAR decided to speak to the fans that make this sport a family event. The television spot titled "Heroes" shows shots of children talking about their dreams. They say they dream of flying, being dangerous, fearless, brave, and a hero, among other things. Halfway into the ad, footage of cars, racing, and drivers are interspersed with shots of the children. It concludes with the dream of wanting to be a racecar driver. Fans of the sport raise their children to be fans as well, so it speaks to those families that bring up their children to view these drivers as heroes and role models.

NASCAR dove even deeper into family loyalty for their Father's Day campaign by getting the fans directly involved through pictures and social media engagement.

"We are all about lineage—fathers and sons, grandfathers. It makes absolute sense for us to put a stake in the ground and own Father's Day for our fans and our brand," Matt Shulman, NASCAR's managing director of marketing platforms, told *Adweek*.

NASCAR asked fans to post their pictures and memories from the races with their own dads to NASCAR's social media sites, using the hashtag #NASCARWithDad. Followers, eager to share their experiences, posted thousands of responses. The posts also served as entries for special prize giveaways. Ten lucky winners received a special Racing Experience Prize Package that gave them the opportunity to drive a stock car with their

fathers. And one grand prize winner landed a ride for two in the Goodyear Blimp over the Homestead Miami Speedway during the Ford Championship weekend.

NASCAR's focus on family is such a simple and effective message and resonates strongly in the New Heartland. It's one that could be used by many other brands as well. By highlighting the family experiences and the bonds created through them, NASCAR has been able to strike an emotional chord with fans and remind them that the races are about so much more than watching cars turn left. This sport, whether watched at the track or on television, has played a part in creating valuable family memories. Congrats to NASCAR for creating a campaign that celebrates those important bonds and connects perfectly with the New Heartlander's core family value!

» More so than the rest of the country, the New Heartland supports their college teams.

» The college game is actually more popular than the professional MLB, NFL, or NBA teams in many areas.

» NASCAR, as the number-one spectator sport in America, offers big opportunities for those brands wanting to connect with consumers at the lifestyle level.

» Youth sports should be on a brand's radar; big business, huge passion, enormous opportunity; consider supporting high school booster clubs as well as schools/teams since they are a key conduit to highly engaged families.

CHAPTER

8

THE GREAT OUTDOORS

THE NEW HEARTLAND +
GREAT OUTDOORS

NEW HEARTLANDERS are **32%** **more likely** to find outdoor activities effective as an advertising element

68%
OF HUNTERS HAVE A HOUSEHOLD INCOME
$50,000+

25% OF U.S. ANGLERS ARE **WOMEN**

56%
OF ANGLERS HAVE A HOUSEHOLD INCOME
$50,000+
▼ ▼ ▼
16% BRING IN **$100K+**

1 IN 10 HUNTERS IS **FEMALE**

1.5 MILLION
FEMALE HUNTERS OVER AGE 16

$	ANGLERS $45B
$	HUNTERS $33B

ANNUAL SPENDING ON GEAR AND TRIPS

20M

GOLFERS
▼
16.5 million
NEW HEARTLAND

10.6 million
NON-NEW HEARTLAND

10M

Illustration 22

The geography of the New Heartland lends itself to some fantastic outdoor recreational opportunities, and we take full advantage. We have everything an outdoor enthusiast could want—mountains, woods, lakes, and plains. The temperatures, landscapes, and culture support some passion-driven activities, but there are a few that stand out as opportunities for brands.

OUTSIDE IN MIDDLE AMERICA

Hunting and fishing are two outdoor sports that have big participation rates in the New Heartland. There are a lot of parallels drawn between the two, and a lot of crossover participants as well. But, they are two very different sports.

I have a lot of friends who are rabid hunters. Hunting season is an understanding. It's understood that they will be deep in the woods on a tree stand or holed up in a duck blind for days at time with no pushback from their significant others.

I've only been hunting once and found that I love every part of hunting except the killing part. The corporation-sponsored dove hunt I was invited to attend was more country club gathering than diehard hunting trip. On the Mississippi/Memphis border, the field we were taken to was seeded with dove food. Fifty or so guests were positioned so we wouldn't shoot each other, at least directly.

A pickup truck bed was literally filled with boxes of shotgun shells and rolled from group to group, replenishing our ammo. Since I was seventeen at the time and had never even held a shotgun, this was a good thing, because I was shooting that thing like I was being attacked by the Taliban. I learned that you're not supposed to follow the bird lower than the tree line when my friend anxiously told me that rule. Evidently, I was peppering the guys on the other end of the field with buckshot via my wild shooting spree. That is not a good way to make friends, I quickly learned. No humans died, so all was good.

Dang, that was fun, though. Then, I noticed I killed eight lonesome doves. And they probably cried, to borrow a Prince line. When it was time to find the birds and ring their necks, I decided it was my first and last hunting trip because that part grossed me out. Plus, since I wasn't going to eat them, I figured it wasn't very responsible to kill for the heck of it. I have huge respect for my friends who are wildly passionate about this sport because of their commitment to preserving the environment and wildlife they love.

When it's hunting season, you'd better get used to seeing a lot of camouflage around. The expansive land areas here make for perfect hunting grounds. Deer hunting is the most popular, with 80 percent of all hunters partaking. The New Heartland represents the largest deer hunting numbers, with the Midwest claiming the top spot—nearly 8 percent of the population.[59]

Check out any sporting goods store, Walmart, or Bass Pro Shop in the New Heartland, and you'll see what I mean. According to the US Fish and Wildlife Service's latest National Survey of Fishing, Hunting, and Wildlife-Associated Recreation Report, hunters spend more than $33 billion a year on gear and trips.[60]

This isn't just a man's game, either. There are 1.5 million female hunters over the age of sixteen.[61] One out of every ten hunters is female. For those who hunt, it's a way of life. And they're bringing their kids up as hunters, too, as hunting is largely a sport of tradition.

There are a few reasons why hunting is still so popular in our region, and they all have to do with geography and culture. Broad landscapes provide a perfect place for agriculture, and sparsely populated areas accommodate growing numbers of wild animals. Population control for deer and other animals that pose a threat to crops or motorists is a big issue in some regions. Culturally, some residents subscribe to a "live off the land" ideology, while others are simply carrying on the recreational traditions learned from previous generations.

Fishing is something that can also be enjoyed year-round in many places. A lot of us love to fish. According to our research, people in the New Heartland are almost 50 percent more likely to have fished in the past two years, compared to people living elsewhere in the country.[62]

According to the Census Bureau, one area of the Midwest in particular—made up of the Dakotas, Nebraska, Kansas, Minnesota, Iowa, and Missouri—boasts 21 percent of its population as anglers.[63] Think about it: One out of every five people in that region fishes!

Women are getting in on the act as well: One of every four fishermen is actually a fisherwoman, which means 7.6 million women fish compared with 22.3 million men.

Stereotype Buster Alert! A particularly intriguing stat on fishing that brands should consider: The wealthier a person is, the more likely they are to fish. Most anglers (56 percent) have household incomes greater than $50,000, with 16 percent of all anglers bringing in more than $100K annually.[64]

And most of this spending is going on in the New Heartland. According to the American Sportfishing Association, we've got eight of the top ten fishing states based on annual expenditures.[65]

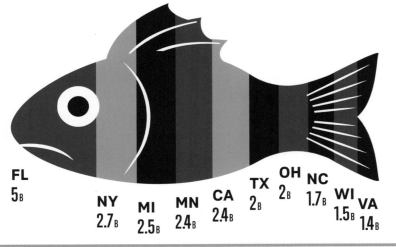

TOP 10 FISHING STATES BY EXPENDITURES ($)

FL
5ʙ

NY
2.7ʙ

MI
2.5ʙ

MN
2.4ʙ

CA
2.4ʙ

TX
2ʙ

OH
2ʙ

NC
1.7ʙ

WI
1.5ʙ

VA
1.4ʙ

Illustration 23   ●● New Heartland   ● Non-New Heartland

New Heartland residents will don a camo jacket one weekend for a hunting trip with buddies, take the family fishing the next weekend, and then grab the clubs to hit the links the next.

According to The National Golf Foundation (NGF), the New Heartland actually plays a little more golf than the rest of the country. The region that makes up the largest percentage of golfers nationwide is in the New Heartland: Wisconsin, Michigan, Illinois, Indiana, and Ohio together are home to 20 percent of all American golfers. The second largest, the South Atlantic at 18 percent, is also in the New Heartland. In total, the NGF reports that 16.5 million New Heartland residents golf, compared with 10.6 million residents of non-New Heartland states.

The two states with the most golf courses shouldn't surprise anyone: California and Florida.[66] But what is surprising is that the New Heartland claims almost double the number of courses found in non-New

Heartland states. Once again, our geography and climate plays to the outdoor enthusiasts' advantage.

Now that you have a better idea how we enjoy the great outdoors, let's discuss how to use this information in your campaigns to connect with us.

Using big-name golfers or high profile outdoorsmen is certainly an option, but you'll probably find more success getting involved on the regional and local levels. These activities are ways that we use to spend time with family and friends. Yes, we follow the big tournaments and have our favorite athletes, but we enjoy participating in the activities ourselves.

Local golf tournaments are a popular way to raise money for many causes in the New Heartland. If your budget is small, sponsorship of these tournaments show your support for our communities, which leads us back to one of our important core values. Your involvement on a local level could be a key factor in gaining a whole new army of brand advocates.

If you're looking for a solution to a national campaign, messaging around these activities/events can help us identify with your brand. As with any effective marketing campaign, consumers are looking for that genuine connection to the brand's story. In looking for a way to better connect with their customers, Dodge Ram took this approach with fantastic results.

CASE STUDY

Ram and Mossy Oak

In a move that shows just how much Dodge understands their customers for the Ram Truck brand, the automaker partnered with Mossy Oak, a camouflage and outdoor lifestyle company, to design a special truck for hunters and fishermen. In Chrysler's research, they found that 30 percent of RAM 1500 owners hunt and 44 percent of them fish, so they decided to create a vehicle that would cater to that large demographic's needs.

In a statement from from Mossy Oak, Executive Vice President Ronnie Strickland noted, "The Ram Truck brand has been a great partner to Mossy Oak. The people there love trucks, but they're also into hunting and fishing and understand that their customers are, too. To have Ram take that relationship to the next level by offering a special Mossy Oak Edition speaks volumes about their commitment to hunters and outdoorsmen and women, and we are extremely proud to partner with them."

Aesthetically, the 2014 Ram Truck gives a great first impression for outdoorsmen with its Mossy Oak Break-Up Infinity camouflage pattern on the exterior wrap and interior accents. With all-terrain tires, a touchscreen navigation system, and four-wheel drive offered standard, outdoorsmen will feel ready for their off-road adventures. There's even a holster for guns and fishing rods built in to the side Rambox cargo areas of the bed. Talk about anticipating your customers' needs!

In this partnership, Ram is also a major sponsor in Mossy Oak-produced television programming that airs on the Outdoor Channel and the Pursuit Channel. They act as a presenting or title sponsor of Hunting the Country, Turkey and Deer Thugs series, Inside the Obsession, and Gamekeepers.

I wanted to highlight this partnership because it's such a bold move for these two brands. Ram did their research to see how their customer base was using their product, and the company created a customized edition for that group. And Mossy Oak jumped in to a business entirely outside their field to help create a superior product for their loyalists.

Not only do outdoorsmen in the New Heartland love this truck, but they also appreciate this level of attention and commitment to their needs. Ram did a great job of taking one of their already popular products and customizing it just enough to super serve the needs of a large portion of their customer base.

» The popularity of hunting and fishing in the New Heartland comes from the abundance of wildlife in an area where tradition is strong. Once a necessity for survival, these handed-down hobbies are now part of the cultural fabric.

» Claiming almost double the golf courses of non-New Heartland states, it's evident that this region takes advantage of the expansive geography and agreeable climate with their clubs.

» To make an impact on this segment, local golf/fishing tournament sponsorships are a great way to support the community.

» Being outdoors is a passion point for New Heartlanders, male and female, young and old.

9 SOCIAL IN THE DIGITAL SPACE

THE NEW HEARTLAND +
SOCIAL MEDIA

ONE MILLION LINKS SHARED EVERY MINUTE

114 BILLION MINUTES A MONTH SPENT ON THE SITE

IS THE
TOP INTERNET ACTIVITY
with **60%** spent on
SMARTPHONES AND TABLETS

2013   2017

5B   10B   15B

500 MILLION TWEETS SENT PER DAY

REVENUES
FROM SOCIAL MEDIA ADS are expected to nearly double from **$6.1 B in 2013** to more than **$11 B by 2017**

INTERNET ADVERTISING WILL MAKE UP **25%** OF AD BUDGETS BY **2015**

EMAILS
WITH SOCIAL SHARES get **158%** HIGHER CLICK-THROUGH RATES

47% OF U.S. ONLINE CONSUMERS MADE PURCHASES BASED ON PINTEREST

The possibilities to connect brands with New Heartlanders are endless when it comes to the digital space, which is why marketers are sometimes overwhelmed when deciding how to maximize this channel. Prior to the Internet, advertising was fairly linear in that ads were placed in TV, print and/or radio, with very few variations available. The power has shifted to consumers and the barrage of brand messaging that impacts their buying decisions have multiplied significantly. Consumers now control the messaging they receive and how/where they receive it. Don Draper and his *Mad Men* cohorts would shudder at this notion.

The tools that help marketers share their story are evolving as well. The classic browser cookie is a staple of targeted advertising as consumers see more relevant messaging based on their previous Internet behavior, although we'll probably see a significant shift away from this approach in the coming years.

Just as all of our devices are increasingly interlinked to create a seamless transition in our online activities, so are most websites we use. And marketers want to know how we're using our devices.

In an article by Tim Peterson in *Ad Age*, he exposes Google's efforts to track users habits on mobile web and their mobile apps, "Google has come up with a way to overcome the ad-targeting gap between mobile web visitors and mobile app users, according to people familiar with the matter."

Peterson explains that Google is testing "a new method of targeting tablet and smartphone users that connects the separate tracking mechanisms that follow what people do on the mobile web and in mobile apps respectively, the people said. Until now, advertisers have usually been forced to treat individual mobile users as two unconnected people, depending on whether they are using a mobile browser or apps."[67]

Facebook noted that a new Altimeter Group white paper that it commissioned shows more than 60 percent of U.S. online adults use at least two devices daily and that more than 40 percent start an activity—such as shopping—on one device and complete it on another.[68]

Think about the last five applications you downloaded or sites you subscribed to. Did you receive the option to sign in with one of your social media profiles? That's because marketers increase their new customer registration by more than 33% percent when social login is an option.[69]

It is now standard for sites to incorporate a range of social channel share buttons. These buttons are not only great for getting new eyes to the site, but it's a veritable gold mine of behavioral research on the types of content with which you choose to engage. Not only do marketers know what customers read, buy or share, they also have access to their age, location, gender, and race. Would you choose to invest your marketing dollars in data derived from a user's cookies or their detailed engagement history? That's exactly why we'll see the continued merging of sites and real-time, preference-driven data.

So as the game changes to morph into the hyper-targeted communication options, you'll want to be sure that you have the right messaging for your ideal customer. That's a minimum expectation for today's savvy digital users.

While time spent with digital media (online, mobile and non-mobile connected devices) surpassed TV viewing for the first time in 2013 that trend is predicted to continue with mobile devices driving the growth.[70] In fact, combining online and mobile devices, U.S. adults are expected to spend five hours forty-six minutes with digital per day in 2014, increasing digital's lead over television to well over one

TIME SPENT PER DAY WITH SOCIAL NETWORKS BY ADULTS

ONLINE 32 mins MOBILE 35 mins TABLET 15 mins SMARTPHONE 20 mins

TOTAL PER DAY : 1 hr 7 mins

Illustration 25

hour per day. Mobile usage alone will increase by 23 percent in 2014, with video content and social networking being two key drivers.

GETTING SOCIAL IN THE NEW HEARTLAND

The New Heartland's behavior online is similar to the rest of the country's. We have a slightly smaller audience than our coastal counterparts, with the Census showing that the populations in the South and Midwest have 2-5 percent fewer homes with access to the Internet. But in terms of how we spend that time online, we're pretty much in line with the general numbers across all states, with one key exception: New Heartland men are 23 percent more likely to have social media recommendations sway purchase decisions than their non-New Heartland counterparts.[71]

Let's look at what gets our attention.

- Social is now the top Internet activity, even surpassing email, with 60 percent spent on smartphones and tablets.[72]

- Facebook absorbs 114 billion minutes a month of consumers' time, and creates seven times more engagement than Twitter.[73]

- Eighty—the approximate number of pages, events, and groups to which the average user is connected on Facebook.[74]

- There's an average of a million links shared every minute on Facebook.[75]

- 271 million monthly active Twitter users sending out more than 500 million tweets per day.[76]

- YouTube beats out any cable network in their reach to U.S. adults in the 18-34 demographic.[77]

- 47 percent of U.S. online consumers have made purchases based on recommendations from Pinterest.[78]

- Adults in the US spend more time on mobile than online.[79]

- Internet advertising will make up 25 percent of ad budgets by 2015.[80]

- Emails with social shares get 158 percent higher click through rate.[81]

- Over the next ninety days, nearly one in five consumers plans to spend more on Internet shopping.[82]

- Revenues from social media ads are expected to nearly double from $6.1 billion in 2013 to more than $11 billion by 2017.[83]

It's not a secret that social media provides a big opportunity for marketers. With about a quarter of our time spent on these sites, it's impossible not to find an audience there. The best part is the level of engagement on networking sites. That Word of Mouth gold becomes more important here. People trust brand recommendations from friends and family.[84] Posts reviewing a product—good or bad—can have an instant effect on hundreds or thousands of consumers' purchasing decisions. Instead of the one-on-one personal recommendation from years past, customers now have essentially been given a megaphone to voice their views and experiences.

Since social media is the number-one Internet activity, it is not surprising that most of them check into social networks on their smartphones rather than desktops. This means that social media will continue to be the most popular web activity. It is time to integrate mobile marketing strategies and target audiences based on location, device, and other niche options for an effective campaign.

Facebook attracts nearly seven times the engagement of Twitter and more than any other social network. Facebook has perfected the multidevice social media engagement strategy, keeping users constantly engaged. Facebook is still the greatest lead generation platform on social media and requires substantial attention while compared to other social networks.[85]

Though it doesn't have quite the same level of participation as Facebook, Twitter posts some pretty large numbers as well. The company reports 271 million monthly active users sending out more than 500 million tweets per day![86] This social platform is great for brands that want to get out quick messaging, make a one-on-one connection with their customers, and draw attention to their other online properties. Users connect with brands on Twitter to get special offers, have a direct line of communication with the brand, and to receive relevant updates from the company. Keep this in mind when developing your strategy for this channel.

Pinterest should be part of your strategy as well. Often considered the "top of the funnel" channel, Pinterest is a strong site traffic driver (for new and potential customers) and is one of the best social media lead generators, making it very attractive to online retailers. Pinterest buyers also spend more money, more often, on more items than any of the other top five social media sites, so engaging your brand with customers with visually dynamic Pinterest boards can be a win. Plus, people trust their Pinterest networks to recommend quality products—in fact 47 percent of U.S. online consumers have made purchases based on recommendations from Pinterest.[87]

Turn social media fans into advocates by equipping and incentivizing them to talk about your brand within their social network. For example, hotel chains such as Radisson Blu and Kimpton Hotels run social media contests to get guests engaged and posting about their properties. Radisson guests can earn free nights by posting travel tips and Kimpton guests earn perks and freebies by mentioning its hotels on social media.[88]

But we see that social media isn't the only place we visit online—shopping and entertainment rounded out the rest of our time online. These statistics are excellent news for marketers interested in creating branded entertainment or streamlining the shopping experience.

As demonstrated by the Experian findings, our time online largely revolves around leisure activities in spaces we create for ourselves. Nobody wants that space interrupted with invasive and irrelevant marketing messages. But, if done right, entertaining and informative content can be a welcome addition to the online experience.

To decide the right approach for your messaging, let's first explore why a person might welcome ads or engage with branded content at all. The key is making sure the message has the highest likelihood of being positively received. The "spray and pray" method of disseminating information, especially via the Internet, is a sure way to kill your message. And nobody purposely incorporates murder into their marketing mix.

KEYS FOR CREATING ENGAGING SOCIAL MESSAGING

I. Incentives: A sale, coupon code, or prize giveaways are fast favorites for consumers looking for a deal. In fact, seven out of ten consumers say digital coupons have a positive impact on affecting purchase decision.[89] But, as I tell my retail clients, the incentives need to provide real value; Ten percent off means nearly nothing on a commodity item. Give them something they can sink their teeth into like a deep discount or gift with purchase. Free shipping has become the norm and is very important in closing sales and competing with others in your space.

2. Emotional Reactions: Those happy customers that were blown out of the water by excellent service or a superior product will share their experience. Likewise so are those unhappy customers. Good or bad experiences with your brand can trigger an emotional response that will spread quickly on digital platforms.

3. Entertainment: Some brands are just known for being funny or entertaining. People want some laughs, a helpful how-to, or insightful writing to read. This is the content that grabs the most attention and is spread socially. Did you watch Felix Baumgartner parachute from outer space in the Red Bull balloon? That was riveting and Red Bull owned it.

4. Good Stories: If your company is spearheading a worthy cause, has an admirable ethos, or encourages local community involvement, you'll find a willing audience to spread your message. These positive stories outside your product brand message can spread like wildfire and not only predispose people to your company, but also build equity in your brand in the most authentic way. People like to be involved with stories that make them feel good.

Keep these points in mind when developing your social strategy for the New Heartland. And don't forget to track your results, which is easy to do with analytics tools and tracking mechanisms readily available. You will have to tweak your tactics to dial in on the results you're looking for, so set up the metrics at the beginning of your campaign.

But remember that the message is still the most important part. Even though the New Heartland shares roughly the same online behaviors as the rest of the country, you'll still need to know the local language to secure an audience.

WHAT HAPPENS IF THEY'RE SAYING BAD THINGS?

No brand is perfect. You can have a million people singing your praises, but there will always be someone who has a complaint. This is the nature of all businesses, and the best thing to do to address negativity is to establish a strong company policy that you can refer to whenever there is an issue. Your brand will have to decide how to respond to customer concerns, whether that is returns and exchanges, accommodating special requests, taking outside ideas, or any number of other inquiries.

With so much time spent on social media, the consumer is starting to turn to channels such as Facebook and Twitter to voice their displeasure instead of handling it more privately with the company via phone or email. This is both a positive and negative consequence for a brand, but with the right approach, consumer displeasure can turn into an opportunity for the brand to educate the public and show their commitment to satisfying their customers.

There are basically four ways to handle a negative comment on social media.

1. Delete it.

2. Ignore it.

3. Offer an apology.

4. Offer a solution.

The first two options can be detrimental to a brand. While deleting a negative comment might seem like the easiest way to get rid of the negative attention, it will often just anger the consumer further that they are being ignored. This could cause them to lash out on other social channels, making the negative comments spread rather than die out. A similar effect can be seen when a comment is ignored.

The best thing to do is a combination of 3 and 4—offer an apology and solution to the complaint. Perhaps the complaint concerns your shipping policy, in which case an apology and explanation of shipping options could be the best response. In the case of an unsatisfactory product, offering a free return or refund might be the best solution. Just remember that your response should be made publicly so that others looking at your page can see that you addressed the issue in a timely and responsible manner. Also, be prepared for others to expect the same treatment—so if you offer a refund for one person, others will expect the same.

Make sure your policies are consistent across the board. In some cases it might be okay to take the conversation to a more private setting. For example, if you are offering an unhappy customer a refund but do not want to set off a chain reaction, respond publicly to their comment and ask them to contact you at a specific email address. This is one of the reasons I always recommend clients hire a professional to produce a social media strategy and plan. A good plan details out what the appropriate steps are when this happens. So, when in crisis, an employee can represent the company properly.

In some cases, the solution might not be clear. For instance, if the complaint is a request for a new product to be produced, there may not be a solution you can offer that satisfies their request. In this case, letting the consumer know that you are listening and taking their suggestions into consideration is best. The consumer wants to know that the brand is listening, and expects to be able to reach them immediately via social channels—so a brand always needs to be prepared to respond immediately when a problem arises.

Stages West is a one-store, western-inspired retailer and e-commerce site that has grown their Facebook audience by almost twenty thousand in the last year. Instead of calling the store to ask a question, several customers send messages or post comments asking about stock, sizing, and more. Stages West has come up with a social strategy that includes constant monitoring and regular posting across all of their social channels.

While most of their engagements are positive, they do on occasion receive critical messages and posts. When addressing any negativity, Stages West starts by offering their sincerest apology and gathering all information possible about the discontent.

One time they received some negative comments about the price point of a brand of boots they carry. Their social media manager listened to the concerned, voiced it to the management team, and together they came up with an appropriate response that reinforced the company's Price Match Guarantee policy. They went back to the customer who had been concerned and asked what they were specifically looking for in a boot. Their boot specialists were then able to come up with several options in their price range and linked the customer to them. This helped the customer see that Stages West had more to offer than they had previously known, and also showcased their attention to customer service, which is one of the characteristics they pride themselves on.

If there is something wrong with your product, you will hear about it on social. If five out of ten posts are the same complaint, then you probably need to do something about your product. And the longer you wait, the more damage you do to your brand.

> *"Nothing will put a bad product out of business faster than a good advertising campaign. Advertising causes people to try a product once, but poor quality eliminates any possibility of a repeat purchase."*
> — Morris Hite, member, Advertising Hall of Fame

Remember that these social media channels are little communities; it would benefit you to treat them as such. They are spaces where you can speak with your customers. Their opinions can be voiced in seconds, so be sure to include them in a dialogue that is respectful and authentic.

Atlanta Showcases Community Pride with #weloveatl

In a grass-roots effort that speaks to the influence and importance of Community in the New Heartland, the citizens of Atlanta are harnessing the power of social media to show just how much they love their city while giving back to it at the same time.

It all started with Atlanta photographer Tim Moxley. While checking out Instagram shots with the #atlanta hashtag, he noticed some great shots that told an interesting story for the city. He decided to take the idea and run with it. He teamed up with three other local photographers, Keith Weaver, Aaron Coury, and Brandon Barr. Together they formed a plan to get the citizens of Atlanta to take pictures of their city and tag them with a #weloveatl hashtag. A select number of those would be picked to hang in a gallery show, with the proceeds from the sales benefiting the Atlanta Community Food Bank.

They began the project by taking pictures of the city, posting them to Instagram, and tagging them with the #weloveatl hashtag. They encouraged their followers to follow their lead and share the idea. They expected to receive a few dozen shots, but instead were blown away when the community answered with more than 5,000 photos in just a month. The team picked 275 shots to be printed and hung at the Youngblood Gallery. The show raised $3,271 for the food bank and brought in more than 1,000 people from all backgrounds to celebrate the city together.

After the overwhelming response, the team knew they had to keep the momentum going. They dreamed up the idea of a mobile gallery that could travel around the city displaying a rotating selection of prints from the photo entries. By launching a Kickstarter campaign, they raised more than $7,500 to buy and brand a bread truck that they could use to take the prints to city neighborhoods and events. Today, more than 75,000 pictures have been posted to Instagram with the #weloveatl hashtag, and

the team has raised enough revenue to fund more than 37,000 meals for the food bank.

This simple, yet fantastic idea that used the power of the community to give back to the community is a perfect example of how the New Heartland operates. Whether it's a big city or a small town, the sense of hometown pride is a theme that resonates throughout. Not only did the Atlanta Community Food Bank benefit from the project, but the city of Atlanta did as well.

» Social engagement is no longer a second-tier marketing choice of whether you do it or not. It must be a pillar of your marketing efforts.

» Your social strategy must be fluid, targeted, and relevant.

» The importance of community in the New Heartland is a top priority. The communities we take part in online are a very important extension of that.

» Both Pinterest and Mobile are game changers in the digital space, so make sure you have your brand well represented .

» Word of Mouth recommendations or criticisms are amplified here. Make sure you have a plan in place for handling the feedback.

KEY POINTS: SOCIAL IN THE DIGITAL SPACE

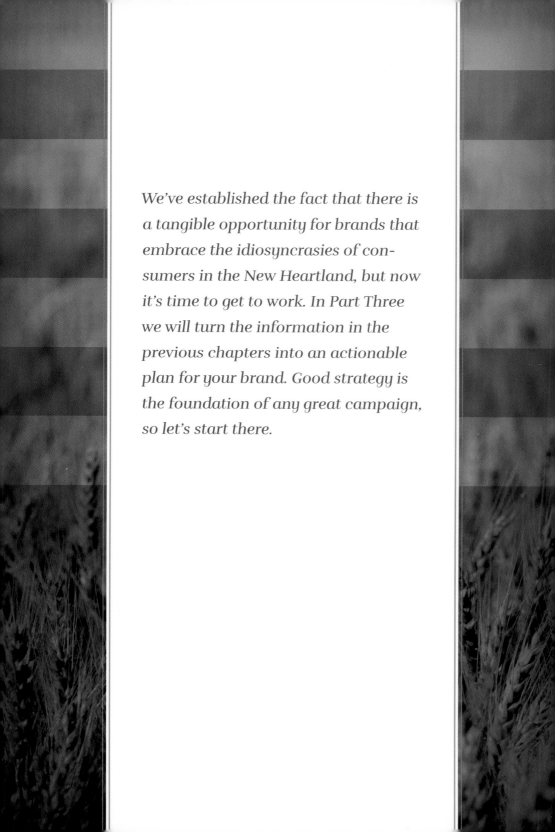

*We've established the fact that there is
a tangible opportunity for brands that
embrace the idiosyncrasies of consumers in the New Heartland, but now
it's time to get to work. In Part Three
we will turn the information in the
previous chapters into an actionable
plan for your brand. Good strategy is
the foundation of any great campaign,
so let's start there.*

PART THREE

DESIGNING YOUR NEW HEARTLAND CAMPAIGN

CHAPTER

10

MAKE SURE YOUR BRAND SPEAKS AMERICAN

The word "brand" has become this ubiquitous term that everyone from entrepreneurs and actors to pro athletes and musicians reference in everyday conversations and media interviews. It has turned into a diluted catch-all that has lost its way and true meaning.

You must understand the meaning of "brand" before you can effectively build one. This is where I always start when I speak at conferences in an effort to set the foundation. Perhaps it's just a pet peeve of mine, but I've heard several agencies talk about how the logo and/or slogan represents a brand. To wit, this directly from an agency's website explaining their capabilities:

"We begin our work by defining that (brand) relationship. Then we clearly articulate it in a logo, color scheme, tagline, typography, photography, illustration and more, so that with just a *quick* glance, people know exactly what the brand is all about."

I don't dispute the extreme importance of a logo, color scheme or typography, but those visual elements alone do *not* tell people what a brand is all about.

There is no shortage of definitions of the word "brand." I've found several thoughtful definitions and believe there are valid variances in how one might come to their own understanding of the word.

"A brand isn't a brand to you until it develops an emotional connection with you."

— Daryl Travis, *Emotional Branding*

"... brands speak to the mind and heart"

— Alina Wheeler, *Designing Brand Identity*

"A brand is whatever the consumer thinks of when he hears your company's name."

— David F. D'Alessandro, *Brand Warfare*

Walter Landor, one of the greats of the advertising industry, said:

"Simply put, a brand is a promise. By identifying and authenticating a product or service, it delivers a pledge of satisfaction and quality."

But to quote branding expert, Colin Bates, this is my favorite:

"A brand is a collection of perceptions in the mind of the consumer."

Here's why I like it:

- This definition makes it absolutely clear that a brand is very different from a product or service. A brand is intangible and exists in the mind of the consumer.

- This definition also helps us understand how advertising works. The purpose of advertising, at its root, is to sell a product, and it achieves this by positively influencing people's perceptions of the product or service.

START WITH SOLID
BRAND STRATEGY

If we can agree that an acceptable definition of the word "brand" is a *collection of perceptions that develop an emotional connection*, then managing those perceptions and emotional connections becomes a massively crucial task in building and protecting brand equity.

This is where logo, color scheme, tagline, typography, and photography become part of the bigger conversation.

Every controllable perception must be kept in sync with the brand strategy.

Without customers, no brand will survive. But a key element that gets frequently overlooked is whether or not a company's employees understand the brand they're supporting. Obvious, I know, but ask yourself if everyone at your company (*everyone*) really understands what you as a brand marketer are doing. Have you tuned them into the strategy and brand essence? I believe everyone from the receptionist to the chief financial officer (yes, especially the numbers people) must be included as you roll out your strategy. They don't need to buy in or even approve of the strategy, but it's in your best interest to cultivate brand advocates from within your organization before you start reaching outside to consumers.

If someone is taking a paycheck from your organization, then they need to be properly educated on the brand's goals. Through this inclusion, you give your employees a guide on how they can better represent your company through their respective roles. More importantly, you give them ownership and skin in the game. They're more likely to pay attention to details and go the extra mile if they're invested, understand the whole picture, and aren't just relegated to "doing their job." That is such narrow thinking. You'll be surprised how much the very act of including everyone in the conversation (at least the topline) will give you a much stronger base from which to build your brand. You are, in fact, creating a culture to nurture your brand from within ... the best place to start.

Let's get down to the basics. As any agency or brand manager worth their salt will tell you, strategy is the backbone of sustainable brand building. It's the roadmap for your brand-equity-building journey. It might require detours, delays, and frequent bathroom stops, but it's the one thing the team can always refer to that will get the brand to its destination.

A rocket doesn't go directly to the moon. It's constantly course-corrected along the way. It's the same with a brand strategy. Without proper preparation, research, and vision, your strategy and your brand are doomed. Take the time to carefully build a strong strategy. Then, be ready to make changes along the way.

Your campaign might have the most brilliant creative, flawless execution, with a dynamic PR team drawing eyes to it, but if the message doesn't resonate with the intended audience and authentically represent your brand's essence, then its effectiveness will be short-lived.

NEW HEARTLAND CONSUMER INSIGHTS:

BRANDS ARE MISSING THE MARK WITH NEW HEARTLANDERS[90]

—Only 4% said ads appeal to their Core Values

—40% said ads rarely appeal to their Core Values

—New Heartland women are nearly 3 times more likely to say they feel overlooked by brands in advertising

A great brand knows where it stands in the marketplace. And it defines that position first and foremost through its Unique Selling Proposition (USP). Your USP clearly tells your target consumers what you do and how you stand out from your competitors.

And it all starts with a solid understanding of your brand. Why your product or service exists, what you do to make life better, how you do it and ultimately who you do it for. Work with your team to develop your USP. Write a simple list of attributes you believe describes your brand. Start with these questions. Be honest.

1.   Why does our brand exist?
2.   What three words best describes our brand?
3.   What are our brand's three core values?
4.   What are the top three perceptions we must control?
5.   What makes our brand totally unique?
6.   What negative perceptions exist (or could exist) about our brand?
7.   How is our brand positioned against the competition?
8.   Do we solve a performance gap or customer problem?
9.   Can we offer proof for the claims we make?
10. Can we condense our USP into one clear, concise, and compelling sentence?
11. Can we deliver on our USP?

Now overlay a second set of questions relating to your brand and its connection to the New Heartland consumer:

1. How do your company's values resonate in the New Heartland?

2. Does your brand team understand the role these values play in buying behavior?
   a. Faith
   b. Community
   c. Family

Illustration 26

3. Out of the Five Channels of New Heartland Access, which ones make the most sense for your brand to use?
   a. Music
   b. Food
   c. Sports
   d. Outdoor
   e. Social
4. What is your brand's reputation in the New Heartland?
5. What New Heartland-specific research have you done?

We've spent a lot of time discussing the importance our Core Values carry and the powerful effect they have on our purchasing decisions in the New Heartland. A brand that not only defines itself as a supporter of the local community, but lives it too, will go a long way in developing loyalty in the New Heartland. Just make sure your brand messaging, regardless of which audience or cultural segment you are targeting, genuinely represents who you are as a company—transparency is key.

Think about SC Johnson. They define themselves as "a family company." This global manufacturer is responsible for a long list of famous brands, with products spanning from household cleaning to auto care. Yet, what they would like for consumers to know first and foremost is that family is the value they hold most dear. That is their brand promise and it is reflected in everything they say and do.

Once you've nailed down the Why, What, and How behind your brand promise, you need to define the Who.

Having read through the first two parts of this book, you've gotten to know the New Heartland a lot better. Are there core values your company should be emphasizing or adopting?

Continuity is a key factor in supporting your brand positioning across all channels. Be sure that online and off, in small regional markets or global ones, your overarching messaging remains consistent. Since all consumers are bombarded with messaging, every touchpoint has to be believable and relate to the way we live our life.

NEW HEARTLAND CONSUMER INSIGHTS:

WHICH STORE IS YOUR FAVORITE TO SHOP?[97]

Walmart fares better with New Heartlanders

WALMART

40%   29%

Target fares better with both

TARGET

42%   48%

New Heartland
Non New Heartland

Down the road, about thirty minutes from my home, is the Jack Daniel's Distillery. It's a point of pride for Tennesseans and can make for an interesting afternoon, if you're up for a free tour of the place. You'll learn about how they make their world famous whiskey, hear about the history of the distillery and laugh at a few of the tales about Jack himself. The stories are the best part, and the company knows it.

As Jack Daniel's senior vice president and managing director, John Hayes told *Marketing Week*, "It's a true story about a real place in Lynchburg, Tennessee. Essentially, what we do is just tell the story about the product, how it's made, the process that makes it a unique whiskey, the people and the place—and a lot of it is about our brand stories over the years."[92]

"People find the story unique, and the consistent manner in which we tell it underscores the authenticity and credibility of the brand. We have proved that the consistent message and story we have is motivating to consumers around the world. It's a big part of our success."[93]

Even though they market to different countries, the message stays the same.

Hayes adds, "You have to evolve with the times, with consumers, and with cultures. How we communicate in China would be different to how we communicate in the UK, but we're still telling a similar story."

A brand's story is the foundation for creating a real consumer connection as well as compelling content. Whether it be the rich history, the ideals of the company, or the lifestyle inspired by your products, every brand has a story to tell.

After you've identified your brand's story, it's time to engage specialists to help craft and deliver your message.

SPECIALISTS ARE SPECIAL FOR A REASON

A big mistake companies often make concerning marketing lies in the assumption that one size can fit all. Today's marketing teams are expected to master traditional media, social media, B2B outreach, Search Engine Optimization (SEO)/Pay-Per-Click (PPC) campaigns, e-commerce, sponsorship activation—and the list goes on. Furthermore, these teams are tasked with reaching multi-dimensional audiences and cultures. The most successful brands understand how to play to the strengths of their in-house marketing teams and know when it's time to call in some outside specialists.

Finding a specialist to fill in the experience gaps on your team is a sign of a mature marketer. Admitting when you don't know the answer is a sign of wisdom. Your team might be a powerhouse of talented experts in their field, but their skills may not translate to leveraging the impact of a culture such as the New Heartland.

The UK retail giant Tesco found this out the hard way.

Tesco is one of the world's largest retailers, employing more than 530,000 people in Europe and Asia. They pride themselves on core values such as: "No one tries harder for customers; we treat everyone how we like to be treated and we use our scale for good."

To continue their aggressive growth in the grocery sector, they looked to expand to the United States with a line of Fresh & Easy grocery stores in 2007. They defined their target market—big box shoppers in America. They conducted extensive research to find out what was important to this group. According to their findings, Americans wanted "fresh, convenient, organic, quality products at a good price from a store that was socially and environmentally responsible."

Tesco took this to mean that the current options on the market simply weren't good enough. They plowed ahead and created more than two hundred beautiful, environmentally responsible Fresh & Easy stores, complete with a splashy marketing campaign. They put stores in Northern and Southern California, Nevada, and Arizona.

It took about six years for the U.S. arm to go bankrupt, forcing a sale to YFE Holdings, Inc. What went wrong here? Well, in an article in *Ad Age*, Jess Neill, strategist at Red Peak Branding said, "Tesco found that Americans want a one-stop shop but still go to many stores. The data wasn't wrong; Tesco's mistake was assuming they understood the context. Its interpretation was that the competition simply wasn't offering a good enough one-stop shop and that a more perfect alternative would succeed.

But within cultural context, there's another explanation. Americans only like the idea of one-stop shopping. And in a car-centric, commuter culture that views shopping as entertainment, they'd rather go to multiple enjoyable stores than one. But they'll still complain about it.

Tesco let research alone guide their strategy and didn't employ a cultural specialist to supplement the data and provide context for the findings. They would have been wise to more fully dive into the American culture and the reasons behind our decisions. All of the exhaustive research they collected was useless without the proper team of specialists to analyze and interpret it.

This is the whole point of this book. In my years in marketing, I've found that the New Heartland remains a massively underserved market. In most cases, we're lumped in with the rest of the country as if there are no regional differences. And sometimes outside marketers targeting regions within the New Heartland simply rely on data without the cultural context. I hope this book provides research that's helpful along with the cultural reasons behind the numbers.

Specializing in the geographic region and cultural segment that I do, my company is often sought out for help in engaging New Heartland consumers. Whether it's a solo project or one worked alongside a brand's ad agency team, we offer an insider's perspective needed to make a good campaign great.

At New Heartland Group, we, too, follow this rule in our own work. As we also work on campaigns that reach beyond the New Heartland, we understand the value of consulting an expert or agency that specializes in a region with which we are unfamiliar. Our job is to achieve our clients' objectives. If that means we can strengthen our work by inviting more people to the table, then we're happy to do it.

Agency ego plays a big role in stunting the growth of brands. How does the tail wag the dog in so many cases? Weak clients allow their over-assertive agencies to control the brand message. This is the wrong combination. Collaboration and respect-with-challenge is the healthiest client-agency relationship.

Mountain Dew Taps the New Heartland with Music and Sports

The Mountain Dew team from PepsiCo approached us to help design and implement a New Heartland strategy to support their national "This is How I DEW" campaign.

Mountain Dew, developed in the 1940's in the hills of Tennessee, was originally created as a moonshine mixer. Its New Heartland origins made it a popular drink in the area, and its champions gave it a reputation for a brand that does things its own way. Mountain Dew enthusiasts self-identify as the "original instigators."

For this specific effort, Mountain Dew were aiming to increase the number of Millennial males who would claim Mountain Dew as "a brand I love," as well as enable their bottlers to dominate their respective markets. They asked us to concentrate on the music portion of the campaign.

Mountain Dew has a rich history in the music scene. They partner with a wide range of acts that align with the brand's reputation for doing things their own way. DEW even has a record label, Green Label Sound, that supports emerging artists in multiple genres.

Country music was the perfect genre to leverage their music heritage while tapping into the brand's New Heartland roots. There are only a handful of artists in country music that would exemplify the "This How I DEW" mentality. After investigating several artist possibilities, we recommended Jason Aldean.

Jason Aldean is one of the top-selling male artists in country music. In addition to his sold-out stadium performances, Aldean is known for doing things his own way.

The "This is How I DEW" campaign was multifaceted and heavily supported by retail, media, digital, and social assets. The foundation

of the campaign was a national, "All Star" TV commercial featuring Lil Wayne, Olympic snowboarder Danny Davis, skateboard sensation Paul Rodriguez, and Aldean.

The key asset that leveraged Aldean's power in the New Heartland and with country music fans was a fifteen-second cut down of the national spot that featured Aldean. This version was made available to regional bottlers to run at their discretion. The "take rate," or number of bottlers who ran the spot in their market, exceeded expectations and helped satiate the bottlers' desire for content relevant to their markets. Most, but not all, of the bottlers who chose to run Aldean's version of the "This is How I DEW" spot were located in the New Heartland.

This is a perfect example of tailoring a national platform to the needs of regional stakeholders without changing the message. This is also the perfect example of "Speaking American" and how to be culturally relevant without altering the overarching brand message.

We were asked to develop concepts for the next iteration of "This is How I DEW." Staying true to the "original instigator" positioning and embracing the deep country roots, we developed the Raw Country platform. Raw Country was all about the original "outlaws" in country music: Willie Nelson, Waylon Jennings, Johnny Cash, Merle Haggard, and David Allan Coe, to name a few.

This unpolished sound attracts listeners of a certain mindset or way of life. Raw Country fans aren't interested in slick, studio-produced albums, but enjoy country music that goes back to its roots—straight back to the honky-tonks.

We designed a strategy that would speak directly to these fans. Plans were made for onsite activation components at shows

and in-store retail locations. We found where our audience lived online and made sure to create content for that space.

The Raw Country platform was manifested in DEW's "Down 'N Dirty Experience" and brought to life with prize giveaways, interactive experiences at shows, and online retail promotions, among other activities.

For this phase of the DEW campaign, we enlisted Raw Country artist, Brantley Gilbert. He is the personification of Raw Country and Down 'n Dirty. He lives it, writes songs about it, and ties it all together in his high-energy, in-your-face, country/rock live performances. DEW supported the campaign through retail, radio and online promotions, on millions of can panels and hospitality events at each of his concert stops. Gilbert also joined fellow DEW ambassador, Dale Earnhardt Jr., in a national TV spot.

As an adjunct to the Brantley Gilbert partnership, we were enlisted to help develop an emerging Raw Country artist platform in conjunction with DEW's Green Label Sound initiative.

The emerging artists platform was designed as a way to promote unsigned acts that carried the Raw Country torch. Brian Davis and Stoney LaRue were chosen because of their authenticity and dedication to doing music on their own terms.

The third representative of DEW's "original instigator" status was Dierks Bentley. The campaign ran in 2014 and leveraged Dierks' eleven number-one singles and his broad appeal to bring the DEW message to Millennials. Tour sponsorship, retail integration, digital media, millions of can panels, a performance at NASCAR's Bristol Motor Speedway, and a tie-in to CMT made the Dierks campaign extremely successful.

Mountain Dew's partnerships with country artists who authentically represented the brand had significant impact with consumers and their bottler partners.

» To achieve maximum results for a national campaign, the overall message doesn't need to change, but the way it's communicated in the New Heartland should be altered, in many cases.

» As consumers are increasingly turning to multiple channels and purveyors of information, be sure that their interaction with your brand remains consistent in story and experience.

» Get to know your customer base beyond static analytics; immerse yourself in their culture to round out your understanding of who they are. Get out from behind your desk and go to a concert, festival, or NASCAR race.

» Rely on the assistance of experts to help you learn about the New Heartland and any cultural segment you want to do business with.

KEY POINTS: MAKE SURE YOUR BRAND SPEAKS AMERICAN

CHAPTER

11

TOOLS TO BUILD A SUCCESSFUL NEW HEARTLAND CAMPAIGN

The marketing buzz term du jour is undoubtedly "Branded Content." And while brands have been producing some form of branded content for more than a hundred years, the approach, strategy, and work itself have taken a measurable turn over the past ten years.

With the omnipresent role the Internet has taken, the marketing game has changed completely. Now instead of brands talking to customers, we all know that we must talk with them. They have complete control over the messages they receive. We find ourselves asking permission to be let in to their spaces, online and off.

Instead of shouting a message that falls on many deaf ears, we have the opportunity to craft quality narratives that tell the story of our brands. That's the mark of good branded content—effectively telling the story of your brand.

BRANDED CONTENT THAT'S REAL LIFE, REAL TIME

In one of the most celebrated branded content efforts, Chipotle's Cultivate campaign found a way to tell the food chain's story in a way that resonated with its customers. Since the beginning, Chipotle supported a farm-to-table approach, emphasizing sustainability. They wanted to not only let their customers know that, but also involve them in a bigger conversation about the food industry in general.

Chipotle's "Back to Basics" animated film showed a farmer with just a few animals on a farm that grew into a massive meat factory. After realizing how bad this practice was, the farmer returned to his roots in free-range farming. The soundtrack is Willie Nelson covering Coldplay's "The Scientist." The spot won the Grand Prix at Cannes in 2012 for the newly created Branded Content category. They spread their message through events and social media efforts that celebrate responsible farming and educate the public on the benefits.

Effectively telling (and retelling) the story behind your brand creates a connection the consumer *needs* to differentiate you from the competition. In the music world, ballads sell the most albums because a listener must invest time and emotion into understanding the story the song is telling. Ballads are also the hardest songs to penetrate the chart because of the time it takes for listeners to connect.

Think of your brand story as a ballad, and tell it with the intention of your consumer relating it to their personal life. Have patience as your story is told and, more importantly, re-told by your consumer. That story needs to remain consistent in all channels. This makes it easier for your agencies, employees, and all stakeholders to protect the integrity of your story, because there's no room for them to interpret it to fit their personal beliefs.

Think of the game of "telephone." You remember it … the game where you sit in a circle with friends and a message is passed along to each person by whispering it in their ear. By the time it makes its way back to the beginning, it has been altered based on what people thought they heard, sprinkled with their own interpretation. This is what happens to your brand story if it isn't told consistently, from the source—you.

The past few years have seen an explosion in high-quality, engaging branded content created to bolster brand equity. Branded Content is not about blatant product promotion. As a *Forrester Research Report* so perfectly puts it, "It is designed to build brand consideration and affinity, not sell a product or service."[94]

A 2013 Mail Online survey found that 70 percent of brands and 77 percent of agencies have developed branded content in the past year and that 69 percent plan to increase their budget for it even more in 2014.[95] So, if you haven't incorporated this tactic, now would be a great time to start!

Because people consume information on multiple devices, ensuring your content is optimized for all devices is required. Your website is the place to start. Responsive website design is now the norm and forces developers/designers to ensure content is visually appealing, copy is concise, the site is easy to navigate, and it incites action for the brand (purchase, social sharing, user-generated content).

Our own New Heartland Consumer Insights Study confirmed that Internet research is very important to purchase decisions, with New Heartland men viewing it as more important than men living outside the New Heartland. These quick stats show just how much time we spend online and how often we switch devices to gather related information (e.g., price matching while in a store).

Creating content consistent with how it's being used by your consumer sounds logical, but it doesn't always happen. Many times, our often siloed corporate structure doesn't support collaboration in this vital marketing tactic. Push to remove the departmental walls in your organization to bring all brand stakeholders together at the beginning of the process to avoid costly fixes and redesigns later.

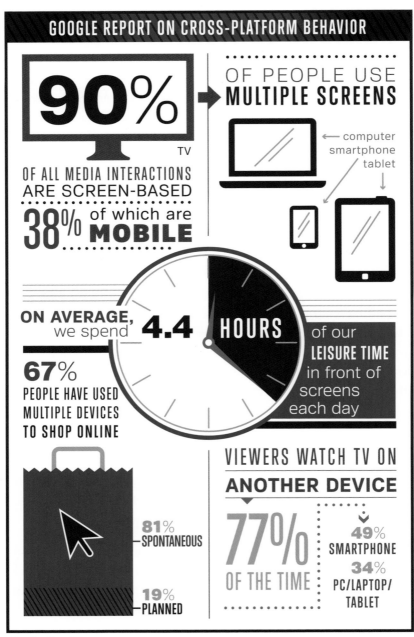

GOOGLE REPORT ON CROSS-PLATFORM BEHAVIOR

90% TV
OF PEOPLE USE MULTIPLE SCREENS

← computer
smartphone
tablet

OF ALL MEDIA INTERACTIONS ARE SCREEN-BASED
38% of which are **MOBILE**

ON AVERAGE, we spend **4.4 HOURS** of our **LEISURE TIME** in front of screens each day

67% PEOPLE HAVE USED MULTIPLE DEVICES TO SHOP ONLINE

81% SPONTANEOUS
19% PLANNED

VIEWERS WATCH TV ON **ANOTHER DEVICE**
77% OF THE TIME
49% SMARTPHONE
34% PC/LAPTOP/TABLET

Illustration 27

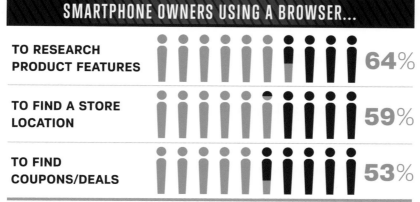

SMARTPHONE OWNERS USING A BROWSER...

TO RESEARCH
PRODUCT FEATURES — 64%

TO FIND A STORE
LOCATION — 59%

TO FIND
COUPONS/DEALS — 53%

Illustration 28

Since we marketers exist to drive sales/revenue, helping our customers through the myriad information options is key. The shopping process, from research to purchase, often employs several screens, with the smartphone quickly becoming the leader.

YOUR STORYTELLING TOOLBOX

Let's go through a few of the many options you have available to help tell your story through content, a.k.a. your toolbox. In telling your brand's story, using the right tool could be the difference maker between seeing average or excellent campaign results.

With today's possibilities, marketers have a plethora of ways to tell their stories. Use the new channels if they make sense in telling your story, not because they are the new shiny toys that have the blogs all aflutter. For example, I'm certain you have heard (from yourself or others) statements such as "Mobile apps are huge right now. We need one!" Does a custom app for your brand make sense? Usually it doesn't. What about other tools?

Once you have a message in mind and your audience defined, reach into your toolbox and find the one to get the job done. Which of these tools will do the best job in getting your customer engaged in your brand's story?

Blogs: Regular blog entries are an excellent way to communicate with your current and potential customers. Providing information about ways to use your product, inviting industry thought leaders to share some insights, or offering a look behind the curtain at your office culture are ways to keep readers connected with your brand. Encouraging feedback and writing with "shareability" in mind will amplify your message. Blogging is an art and goes back to our discussion about using specialists in their field.

Video: There's such a wide range of uses for video that the possibilities are almost endless. Whether used for instructional or entertainment purposes, this tool can paint a very colorful picture that other forms cannot. We are visual creatures, and video ranks at the top of shareable content. Invest in video.

Events: The best part of partaking in an event is the personal contact you have with attendees. Invest in hiring trained brand ambassadors that will connect dots between an event sponsorship and your products' attributes. Face-to-face engagement is key. Signage alone doesn't deliver the value you need.

> **NEW HEARTLAND CONSUMER INSIGHTS:**
>
> NEW HEARTLANDERS ATTEND MORE LIVE EVENTS[96]
>
> —22% More Likely to attend at least 3 live music, sporting or NASCAR events a year compared to non-New Heartlanders

Mobile apps: As apps have exploded in popularity in recent years, the market is completely saturated by some absolutely fantastic offerings and some that just take up space. Apps have been a game changer for how we spend our time and organize our lives. Remember that when you create an app, you're asking for real estate in a space that already competes for a person's attention by the hour. What value can you add that can make their life easier, more organized, or entertaining?

In an article on SmartInsights.com, marketing consultant Susanne Colwyn wrote, "Consumer preference for mobile apps vs. mobile sites should also be thought through as part of mobile strategy. This data from Nielsen on mobile media time shows the consumer preference for mobile apps, which account for 89 percent of media time in mobile from the use of the most popular social network, email, and news apps."[97]

Print: Magazines, newspapers, direct mail, and free standing inserts (FSI), still have the ability to reach a large audience. The amount of print we recommend as part of our client's media strategy has greatly declined, but not totally disappeared.

Microsites: For a campaign that requires a web-heavy interaction, consider building a microsite. You'll be able to gather more direct response results and have free reign with design elements without altering your current brand's website.

Newsletters/E-blasts: Brand loyalists love newsletters and emails for company information, such as sales and new product alerts. There are some fantastic (and affordable) newsletter builder sites today that give you beautiful templates and offer analytics that provide insights on what your subscribers enjoy or pass up. We use Emma to distribute e-blasts to our client's affinity groups; a very efficient and cost-effective service.

Infographics: Probably the best thing to happen to statistic enthusiasts in the recent decade, these good-looking charts help us understand the numbers in a much more aesthetically pleasing way. A well-designed and informative infographic is also a great way to get your findings and/or brand story shared.

Webinars/webcasts: This medium is perfect for a company that would like to produce regular episodes of entertaining or informative content for their clientele to watch (and share) at their leisure.

White papers: If you're a B2B company, you're probably familiar with the value of a good white paper. These reports give authors or companies a chance to stand out among peers and share their research at the same time.

Games: The gaming industry is seeing a huge increase in brand partnership. Advertising is running rampant with placement in games on cell phones, home console systems, and Facebook apps. Some brands create unique games that incorporate their products. As long as the involvement is unobtrusive and fun, players/consumers don't seem to mind.

Social media channels: As a dominant method for interacting with customers in real time, brands see tremendous value in creating profiles on top social sites. The trick is having an administrator who not only understands which ones benefit your brand the most, but also how to manage them, as well. You must be committed to using social channels to create an ongoing dialogue with your consumers.

CELEBRITY ENDORSEMENTS AND SPONSORSHIPS

In my experiences, one of the areas that I've found to be very successful in brand engagement for the New Heartland is event sponsorships and celebrity endorsements. As my agency has worked for years to pair brands with the right celebrity endorsers, I'll explain the process a bit to unveil how this works for anyone unfamiliar.

Given the right brand-celebrity partnership, the results can be significant. The goal of these relationships is to leverage the celebrity's status and fan base to bring more (or different) attention to the brand while increasing sales, building equity, driving engagement, and reinforcing the authenticity of both brands.

I've put together dozens of brand-artist/athlete partnerships and event sponsorships over the last twenty-seven years including Verizon/Beyonce, Taylor Swift/Yahoo-Pepsi Smash, Blake Shelton/Pizza Hut, Jason Aldean/Mountain Dew, Lady Antebellum/Lipton, Elvis/Reese's and Dale Earnhardt Jr./Elvis Presley Enterprises. I highly recommend these partnerships ... for certain brands.

However, not all brands should be in the celebrity endorsement business. You know the brands I'm talking about—those painfully forced and unbelievable celebrity relationships. It's just awkward. For example, did anyone else cringe when they saw the Hulk Hogan/Troy Aikman Rent-A-Center commercials, or was it just me? Did anyone think Tiger Woods actually drove a Buick? Did Paris Hilton's car wash/strip tease entice anyone except a fourteen-year-old boy to eat a Carl's Jr./Hardees hamburger? Bret Michael's (lead singer of rock band, Poison) "Pets Rock" collection of pet apparel and accessories featured at Petsmart ... enough said.

We've all seen the downside of bad brand-celebrity endorsements and the negative effects an endorser's personal life can have on brands. Since the proliferation of social media, TMZ, and the like, every celebrity must be "on" all the time, making the chances for gaffes that would reflect poorly on the brand more prevalent than ever.

The idea of tying a brand to the equity of an artist/athlete usually comes to life during some iteration of a brand planning session. In many cases, the strategy to leverage that celebrity relationship isn't created until after the talent is secured, which may lead to skewed expectations on both sides. To be real, many times celebrities are chosen based on who the brand team wants to meet rather than shared brand characteristics. It's a train wreck waiting to happen, but very common, nonetheless.

There are so many important factors to consider when putting brands and celebrities together. The merging of two distinct, unique brands takes careful planning and cat-like agility to handle the inevitable mid-campaign adjustments.

Choosing the right partner is the difference between massive success (Michael Jordan/Nike; David Beckham/H&M; Ron Burgundy-*Anchorman* 2 (Will Ferrell/Dodge) and oh-crap-we're-screwed (O.J. Simpson/Hertz; Chris Brown/Got Milk and Doublemint, Alec Baldwin/Wegman's Food Market). We use a process that mitigates the oh-crap scenarios as much as possible. It's comprised of many layers of research steeped in deep relationships and experience in the entertainment and sports industries. At the end of the day, we're dealing with human beings, so all the vetting in the world doesn't guarantee a successful partnership, but it sure increases the chances.

NEW HEARTLAND CONSUMER INSIGHTS:

FAVORITE ARTISTS AMONG NEW HEARTLAND WOMEN[98]

1. Luke Bryan
2. Eagles
3. Beatles
4. George Strait
5. Carrie Underwood
6. Blake Shelton
7. Michael Buble
8. Rolling Stones
9. Neil Diamond
10. Celine Dion

Lipton Iced Tea got it right when they enlisted Lady Antebellum to bring their "Drink Positive" campaign to life. Mountain Dew also nailed it in their "This is How I DEW" campaign, featuring a star-studded cast including Lil Wayne, Jason Aldean, Mac Miller, Dale Earnhardt Jr., Paul Rodriguez, Theotis Beasley, and Danny Davis. As previously noted, country music worked so well for DEW, that they added country stars Brantley Gilbert and Dierks Bentley to carry the torch.

While *Forbes*'s "World's Most Powerful Celebrities" list shows who is getting the most attention and biggest paychecks, the celebrities who add value to a mutually beneficial brand-celebrity relationship carry the most power in my book. The *Forbes* list changes each year, but celebrities like Taylor Swift, Beyoncé, and Blake Shelton offer continuity and consistency to brands in the way they conduct their business as a celebrity.

Blake Shelton's ability to make every person he meets feel like they're a good friend, Beyoncé's down-to-earth demeanor, and Taylor Swift's authenticity are attributes that give these celebrities the real power. Brands strive to enter into relationships with this kind of celebrity where the chances of seeing the person they paid millions on the front page of a tabloid are slim.

A celebrity must share similar core values with the brand they're endorsing. Consumers know when the relationship is forced. Instead of having a positive effect, the consumer could view the brand negatively. Celebrity power is subjective, but for my client's money, power is ultimately measured by increased sales and an authentic representation of their brand.

The Blake Shelton and Pizza Hut partnership is a perfect example of shared values and a genuine connection. Pizza Hut was drawn to Blake's massive popularity as a judge on *The Voice* and as a country music superstar. Even more appealing is his approachable nature and his what-you-see-is-what-you-get personality. Additionally, Shelton has a deeply rooted affinity for Pizza Hut, and he tells the story about hanging out at the local Pizza Hut as a teenager in his Oklahoma hometown. From top to bottom, this brand-celebrity partnership made sense.

We were asked by Pizza Hut to engage Shelton's services. We were retained to activate the partnership through a variety of duties including TV/point of sale production scheduling, creative approvals, and his tour "meet and greets." Pizza Hut's ad agency, McGarry Bowen, did an excellent job creating a campaign that leveraged Shelton's celebrity status and overall congenial nature to launch a new line of barbecue and bacon stuffed crust pizzas. The campaigns were supported by a significant traditional and digital media spend, national TV spots, and in-store presence.

Big money is being spent in event sponsorships and celebrity endorsements. *IEG Sponsorship Report* estimates brands will shell out more than $20 billion in sponsorships for 2014.[99] This number has risen over the last few years, indicating that brands are seeing big returns from these partnerships.

We've discussed some of the key areas where brand-loyal New Heartland consumers can be reached. But many companies new to the sponsorship arena don't know where to begin.

When we receive a call from current or prospective clients looking for ways to leverage a celebrity, we always start by asking what their ultimate objective is. Increasing sales isn't always the answer we get. Supporting a certain initiative, building brand equity, or "the CEO is a fan" are some of the responses. Once we understand the objective, we request a brief (overview) on the scope of the project. Included in the brief is what assets the brand can leverage to support the celebrity partner. Media, retail integration, and digital/social support are the most common.

Allocating the brands' media/promotional assets will have a significant effect on the cash required for the celebrity's fee. We've saved clients millions in celebrity fees by leveraging their media assets.

Understanding what motivates the artist/celebrity is the key in making deals that are truly mutually beneficial.

Not every celebrity is motivated by large cash fees. The smart ones leverage the noncash value their brand partner offers, such as promoting them in non-traditional retail or digital channels. That is the secret to successful brand-celebrity partnerships; knowing the key trigger points for each partner and having the ability to satisfy the respective needs.

BEST PRACTICES FOR CELEBRITY PARTNERSHIP/SPONSORSHIP SUCCESS

Incorporating celebrity partnerships into your marketing plan can be a sure way to get your brand noticed, but a lot of factors go into making sure the exposure you get is positive.

Define Your Objectives

Enhancing brand visibility, increasing sales, educating consumers on the benefits of your product, launching new products, and increasing distribution via retail promotions are a few reasons companies look for the help of high-profile individuals or events. Communicating what you hope to achieve will help your brand and creative teams design a more-targeted message, while assisting your talent in understanding the desired results of the partnership.

You'll also need to dial into what audience you're trying to reach and the shared fan base your celebrity partner brings. One of the mistakes that companies make is trying to be everything to everyone. Sure, you can find a spokesperson with universal appeal, but when your goal is to change the behavior or opinion of certain consumers, it's necessary to choose someone that inspires action. There are very few global celebrities that are relevant in all territories. It's better to own a particular consumer segment than dilute the impact of the investment in your celebrity partner by being too broad in your targeted reach.

Measure Everything: Key Performance Indicators (KPI's)

Sure, it's intuitive to talk about measuring the impact of these partnerships, but you'd be shocked to know how few brands actually do it. Once the objectives are determined, a baseline of Key Performance Indicators (KPI) should be established. Aggregating the impact the celebrity relationship has on incremental sales, earned/paid media impressions, and social engagements are a few indicators that paint a broad picture of the campaign's success.

Go Direct to the Celebrity

Celebrities have a few layers of "people": personal managers, business managers, booking agents, publicists, record companies, et al. We've found the most cost-efficient way to acquire talent is by dealing directly with the target celebrity's personal manager. Many brands will employ a talent-acquisition agency that will then call booking agents such as Creative Artists Agency (CAA) or William Morris Endeavor (WME). Or the brand might reach out to a music artist's record label or publicist. These tactics add unnecessary layers between the brand and celebrity while driving up costs through additional commissions. There are exclusive representation arrangements where the only way to book the celebrity is through a CAA or WME, which is fine. They do an excellent job in those instances.

Record labels have gotten into the sponsorship business lately as well, because their core business of selling records has deteriorated significantly. Record labels have entered into "360" deals with artists that allow them to share in previously sacred revenue streams such as merchandise sales, ticket sales, sponsorships, and music publishing.

All this is to say, the brand needs to be as close to its celebrity partner as possible. This is critical, especially when an additional service or request outside the contract is made to satisfy an unforeseen brand need (i.e., additional meet and greet passes in the corporate HQ market). This happens with *every* deal we've ever done. With a relationship that's not complicated by several layers, these requests often are satisfied.

Consider Their Values

The most important thing in deciding who to work with is finding a celebrity whose values align with your brand. This is a partnership, so when you hire a spokesperson or endorser, you are telling your potential customers that this person represents your company, ideas, and values. Dig deep into your partner's background and don't take their representative's word for it ... do your own due diligence, or get someone who knows the entertainment landscape to help you. The last thing you want to find out (via TMZ) is that your new celebrity partner uses a competitor's product in their personal life or beats their girlfriend.

Think Long Term

It's tempting to team up with the hot artist, athlete, or actor du jour in hopes of tapping into some of that publicity that emanates from their every move, but you'll want to consider whether the partnership will benefit you in the long term. As the face of your brand, every move they make is a reflection of your brand positioning. And with a high-profile figure, that image is one that might not be forgotten soon. We can thank the Internet for that.

On more than one occasion, I've had to advise clients on avoiding partnering with the hot act of the day. In one case, the client was convinced it was the right move (based on advice from a very junior member of the brand team), but they weren't aware of what was happening internally at the acts' record label; the fact that they were changing managers and there was strife among the members of the group. Those facts, coupled with knowledge that consumers were burned out on the act, didn't make for a good combination. Thankfully, the client didn't do the deal and the act they wanted will be featured on the "where are they now" lists in a couple of years.

Consult an Expert

Your advertising agency is brilliant at what they do, but if they don't have deep, personal experience in the entertainment/sports/celebrity space, then you're putting your brand on a slippery slope that could lead to PR damage control. Many people claim to have this experience but few actually do. Calling a record label or booking agent on your behalf to find what talent is available puts your brand on *their* agenda. That's the wrong side of the agenda. Your brand should be driving the conversation and not be at the mercy of someone else's priorities. I see this happen all the time. Brand managers often get stuck in bad celebrity relationships, overpaying someone who doesn't align with their brand and causing more ill will than positive traction.

Make sure that whoever is representing your brand with talent understands the needs of all stakeholders. Don't trust this extremely important piece of your strategy to a member of the brand team because "they know music." I've seen countless deals come to a miserable end, leaving bad feelings at every level, because the wrong person was trusted with overseeing a celebrity relationship. You will spend more money on damage control and take years off your life dealing with the fallout if you don't enlist an expert.

Has the person doing your celebrity deals ever spent the night on a tour bus? Have they been on the sideline at pro sports events? Do they know their way around backstage at a concert? Can they have a normal conversation with a global superstar?

The biggest question: Are they starstruck or a fan? If so, use someone else.

Agree on Common Goals

Once you have found someone who proves to be a good match, discuss your objectives. It's fruitless, in any business deal, if a partner does not share your end goals. And that's what this is—a business deal. You'll realize that when the contracts come out the day before a photo shoot or production day to determine what the celebrity will/won't do as part of their commitment. Those are not fun conversations.

By agreeing on desired results, for both parties, you can then figure out the best course of action. Remember, your new partner has his or her own goals for this deal. Whether they're looking to widen their appeal through your solid reputation or hope to reach more fans through the opportunities that extra funding can provide, you need to be sure that their needs are covered as well. As Henry Ford so eloquently put it, "If everyone is moving forward together, then success takes care of itself."

Over the course of our client's national campaign using a well-known music artist, the artist was releasing a new album. Not part of the contract, both parties agreed that leveraging this event was mutually beneficial. The brand promoted the album release through their non-traditional music channels and the artist cross-promoted the brands' product through his massive fan base. This is a perfect example of how deals should work even after the contract is done.

Stay Close to the Deal

When the deal is done and the checks have been written, brand managers typically shift their focus to the other fifty plates they are spinning. This is where doing a deal without the unnecessary layers really pays off. You'll be able to stay involved to make the necessary adjustments and last-minute decisions to ensure a successful campaign. Go on the road to experience what your celebrity partners' fans are experiencing. You don't have to be a fan of that artist to see the impact they're having on your consumer. It's a great feeling to see your brand come to life through your consumers' eyes as they interact with your celebrity partner. This is where the rubber meets the road.

Lipton Iced Tea's "Drink Positive" Campaign Featuring Lady Antebellum

Here's a great case study as an example of how brands connecting with music can have a big impact on the New Heartland.

Lipton Iced Tea was looking to team up with a music act for their Drink Positive campaign. They needed a group that represented their upbeat message and wide appeal as well as the product's health benefits. Lady Antebellum fit their needs perfectly.

The trio is known for their blended melodies, thoughtful songwriting, and approachable personalities. This six-time Grammy Award-winning group is very rooted in their New Heartland values, which Lipton Iced Tea saw as a great asset.

Regarding the partnership, Lady Antebellum's manager at the time, Gary Borman, told *Billboard*: "We've been involved in many [deals]. Some have succeeded and some have failed. But the Lipton people have been so respectful of the band's brand that it made it really easy to marry these two cultures."

For the campaign, my team and I vetted many options before recommending Lady A. We facilitated the relationship, oversaw all contract negotiations, and served as a liaison between the brand, their twelve agencies, and the talent. We coordinated artist participation in two TV commercial productions, radio, PR, and the point-of-sale photo shoot. We oversaw creative approvals and negotiated music licensing. We activated Lipton Iced Tea's involvement in the Lady A tour, including VIP meet and greets, and the backstage "Lipton Lounge."

This integrated campaign hit on all cylinders: two television commercials, an exclusive web series, iTV content, social media engagement, in-store promotions, a comprehensive PR strategy, event-driven sampling, cause marketing, and tour sponsorship.

CASE STUDY

The campaign was extremely successful, generating nearly one billion digital and PR impressions and more than one billion TV impressions. This doesn't include the millions of impressions generated through a very large retail footprint.

Lady Antebellum was a great fit for the Lipton Iced Tea brand. For example, members of Lady A have vivid memories of drinking Lipton Iced Tea after church at their grandmother's house. The partnership was measurable and very successful with the bottler groups. The brand and artist values aligned, and the creative execution made it an authentic and relevant campaign. By employing one of the Five Channels of Access, Lipton Iced Tea was able to appeal to a national, as well as New Heartland, culture with this engaging campaign.

KEY POINTS

» Understanding what motivates your celebrity partner is the key in making deals that are truly mutually beneficial.

» Use an expert to build and manage brand/celebrity partnerships.

» When considering partnering with a high-profile individual, remember that he or she is, in fact, a partner. You'll want to consider not only your short-term campaign goals and long-term brand goals, but their objectives, as well. A symbiotic relationship works much better than a one-sided deal.

» Be consistent in telling your brand's story, using the rights tools, voice, and channels.

» As consumers are increasingly turning to multiple channels for finding information, be sure that their involvement with your brand remains consistent in story and experience across all devices.

CHAPTER

12 PUTTING IT ALL TOGETHER

This is the big "put it all together" chapter, where we take all those bits of knowledge about building a brand with America's most powerful cultural segment and help you apply them to a plan for your brand. You've met us New Heartlanders, understand the role our core values play, and have a good idea as to where we spend our time and/or dollars. Now let's talk about what you can do to make this all relevant and valuable in developing campaigns and messages that engage us, and build loyalty that will last far beyond any single campaign.

THE PROCESS FOR CONNECTING WITH THE NEW HEARTLAND

I believe that building brands in the New Heartland cannot be accomplished from the forty-second floor of a Manhattan high-rise or in a sprawling cubicle office system on the West Coast. I've seen big and small agency creative teams on the coasts try to do this time and time again, and it is destined to miss the mark with the New Heartland.

In order to truly understand the New Heartland consumer, brand strategists and marketing decision makers must immerse themselves in our lifestyle—or hire brand experts who do. It's vital to understand our heritage; where our loyalty stems from; how values impact our buying behavior; and how we discover and engage with products.

In the New Heartland, brands are built at the dinner table, at church gatherings, in the garage, out in the fields, on the production line, at concerts, on the golf course, at soccer practice, and on the front porch after five o'clock. They are passed down from generation to generation, like family heirlooms and treasured recipes. Men drive a certain type of truck because that's what their father drove, and their grandfather before them. Moms buy certain household products because they are the ones their moms used.

Building brands in the New Heartland doesn't come from a focus group or a survey; it stems from deep roots and a heritage that is held close to our hearts. To understand this passion and loyalty, you must find a way to live and breathe it every day.

THE FIVE STEPS FOR MARKETING TO THE NEW HEARTLAND

Let's break this down using the same general process you may already use when defining your brand's marketing strategy, only I'll help you approach your campaign from a New Heartland point of view. Here's the process I use when building a brand campaign:

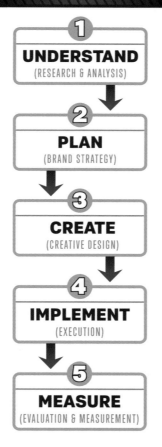

Illustration 29

Many times, simplifying the process and asking questions during each step can lay the foundation for some truly great customer dialogue, which is key to engaging with consumers in the New Heartland. Carefully consider these steps. Just be sure to be diligent about the message your brand is sending and the reasons behind it, particularly when filtering it through core values for New Heartland authenticity.

Get to know your intended audience. There are many subcultures and unique connections within the New Heartland, as well as disconnects by age, geography, religion, gender, and more. Solid research among your core target audiences prior to developing the brand strategy is critical to success. List your brand attributes and values that the New Heartland target market would find appealing, and be equally aware of what they would not find appealing.

We believe the first step of research should be focused on a singular goal: understand current brand perceptions—both positive and negative—and establish a foundation on which to build the brand strategy within the New Heartland.

In this book, we've shown you where New Heartland consumers spend their time and what's important to them, so now it's up to you to determine what messaging and tone would resonate with them. Profile the cultural filters of the New Heartland consumer and know how they will impact perceptions of your brand.

Use research as baseline in your strategic thinking as you build your brand plan. Think through the insights to determine foundational components that must be represented and reinforced in your strategy. Think about core values and lifestyle channels, and other nuances that make the New Heartland consumer unique and likely to engage with your brand. This is the time to lay out a strategy that will help your target consumer to discover the brand, experience the brand, engage with the brand, and ultimately advocate for the brand.

Outline who you are reaching, what you would like this group to know about your brand, and what results you are hoping to achieve. The strategic plan will provide a roadmap to affect emotional and rational drivers of desired behavior—just what will it take to get the New Heartlander to experience and become loyal to your brand? A great brand is only as good as its brand strategy, so consider such elements as:

- Development of the brand platform: Brand promise/essence, brand attributes, brand values/behaviors, and brand voice.

- Analysis of target audiences, key influencers, and existing and desired brand perceptions.

- Statement of key differentiators, based on a SWOT (strengths, weaknesses, opportunities, and threats) analysis.

- Development of key brand messaging and positioning statements by target audience/ influencer group.

- Development of strategies and tactics that reach the New Heartlanders where they are in their daily lives, resonate with their key core values, and authentically build a trusted relationship.

- Establishing goals and objectives and defining short- and long-term measurable results.

CREATE
(CREATIVE DESIGN)

Now the fun really begins as you create a fully integrated campaign with your key brand messages, developing tools, and assets that will reach the New Heartland consumers. Keep top of mind that the

BUILDING A BRAND CAMPAIGN THAT SPEAKS AMERICAN

- Make sure your creative team knows the role that faith plays in buying behavior in the New Heartland. Don't discount and pander to these strong beliefs, but respect them. And remember—religion is not part of this conversation. Also, being faithful in the New Heartland doesn't necessarily equate to being politically or socially conservative.

- Check that the values of your company and brand are authentically communicated in the tone and messaging of your campaign, as New Heartlanders will need to have faith in not only your product, but also your company itself.

- If faith plays a role in your company culture, be transparent about that with New Heartlanders. This will make them more likely to build brand trust and advocacy.

- Be prepared to stand firm on your brand's core beliefs and what it represents, even in the face of controversy.

- Speak the local language and dialect. Enlist local voice-over talent to ensure you're not mispronouncing words in your radio/TV spots.

New Heartland cultural segment is defined by a way of life, not a demographic, a psychographic, or just geography. Remember, you don't need to change your brand message, just the way it's delivered. Think core values of Faith, Community, and Family as you create your brand storytelling tools.

Here is a summary of key tips to guide your creative team and ensure your branding campaign does in fact Speak American.

- Remember that "Hometown" is more than where we live or grew up ... it's a huge part of who we are. Factor that into your creative story.

- Make sure your campaign targets family units, not just individuals, as the family is the foundation of the New Heartlander's identity and number-one source for product recommendations. Remember P&G's big scoring "Thank You, Mom" campaign.

- New Heartland family traditions involve brands, and loyalty to a brand can be passed through multiple generations and extended families. Find a way to connect your brand with traditions that New Heartlanders hold near and dear.

- Choose the right music that connects the New Heartlander with your brand. This is a proven brand-building tactic—from jingles and audio tracks, to full-blown artist sponsorship/branded entertainment campaigns.

- Remind your creative team that America is the number-one brand for New Heartlanders, so connect your campaign with America where it makes sense. If your products are "Made in America," fly that flag high in your New Heartlander campaign!

MAXIMIZING THE NEW HEARTLAND LIFESTYLE CHANNELS

- Find ways to connect your brand with community—volunteer groups, youth sports, schools, neighborhoods, local causes, and local businesses. The more New Heartlanders experience your brand in their local community circles, the faster you'll earn their trust.

- Engage New Heartland thought leaders and influencers such as business, community, and political leaders, and bloggers and journalists, in ways that are relevant to your brand. They are your key to getting an invitation to Sunday dinner.

- Remember that you have to earn trust to become a worthy topic of conversation in the New Heartlander's communities, so step up and speak out with consistency, transparency, and honesty.

- The importance of Word of Mouth throughout the New Heartland family network can't be overstated. If you can turn a New Heartland family into a brand advocate, the success of your brand will exceed your wildest expectations.

- Country music is tops with New Heartland and non-New Heartland women alike. New Heartland men love their country music but are huge fans of rock, as well. Find ways to connect your brand with music artists and their fans.

- With us, food means connection to community, a reason to socialize, and a way to bring family together. Find ways to have your brand invited to the dinner table, backyard cookouts, potluck casserole socials, and tailgate events.

- Connect your brand with New Heartland brand fanatics through the sports that personify the New Heartland's core values—college sports (especially football) and auto racing.

- Youth sports from football and soccer to dance and cheerleading have exploded and offer a great way for a brand to reach New Heartland families. Your brand can be a big help to time-and-money-stretched families with scholarships and sponsorships, while promoting healthy lifestyles and supporting the local community.

- Hunting, fishing, and golfing are not only big business in the New Heartland, they are big family activities and enjoyed by men and women alike. Tying in with these great outdoor sports will also connect you to New Heartland families.

- Leverage the power of sponsoring local events/tournaments.

- When you engage with the New Heartlander in the digital/social media space, make sure you are committed to real-time, interactive, and relevant conversation.

- Social media platforms for New Heartlanders are just an extension of their community—a core value they hold dear. Build in ways to earn an opportunity to become part of those conversations.

Take your research and search your workbench for the best tools for the job—video, blogs, social media, digital platforms, and sponsorships. Match your brand promise with creative messaging that resonates with your New Heartland consumer. Then bring it to life through powerful imagery and engaging content.

Think about the potential of having a celebrity voice attached to your brand. Think about designing campaign tools and brand assets that will create engagement and real relationships using the vast array of social media and digital platforms. Make sure the work fits your own values. And don't be afraid to take chances—just keep it real.

4

IMPLEMENT

(EXECUTION)

Launch your creative work with gusto and create a brand platform that allows New Heartlanders to discover, experience, engage, and ultimately advocate for your brand. Remember that your plan must aim to build deep consumer relationships in order to build a sustainable brand within the New Heartland. Make sure you are focused on the key lifestyle channels and meet them there.

Create continuity and collaboration around the campaign—internally, with loyal customers, and with new audiences. As you execute your campaign, take New Heartland insights into consideration.

MEASURE
(EVALUATION & MEASUREMENT)

Check the success and failures of the campaign. Course correct along the way to maximize what's working best, and minimize what's not. Compare your results against your first-step goals. If you didn't achieve what you had hoped, check your list to see where you went off course. Remember it is not the short-term brand discovery you are after, but the long-term brand advocacy that will generate your greatest return on investment.

Here are just a few of the ways you can track, measure, and evaluate your campaign throughout the process:

- Incremental sales
- Stakeholder/influencer engagement
- Customer reviews
- Website traffic
- Social media mentions, sharing, and engagement
- SEO rankings
- Advocacy and influencer endorsements
- Internal and external brand recognition

In working on your New Heartland campaigns, use this book during the process. Let it help you research your audience, learn the spaces where they connect to your brand, and get ideas from those brands that engage well with the New Heartland. Let's take a look at one final case study and see just how well this process works.

CASE STUDY

Toyota Texas Bass Classic

For our final case study, we're going to take you to a fantastic New Heartland campaign that has it all—appeal to our Core Values, several Channels of Access, and flawless execution. We'll walk it through our Five Steps for Marketing to the New Heartland to examine the process from start to finish. This case study is a look at the Toyota Texas Bass Classic in Quitman, Texas.

Each year, thousands of fishing fans descend upon Lake Fork to watch world-class anglers compete in a three-day catch-and-release tournament. The tournament takes place in the middle of a huge festival that brings great food and family-friendly entertainment to the local community. Brands, big and small, get in on the action as well take advantage of reaching such a valued group of attendees.

The Texas Parks and Wildlife Department needs significant funding to preserve and maintain natural resources of Texas, as well as provide hunting, fishing and outdoor recreational opportunities for Texans. They created a festival to help them do just that.

The audience to reach here is smack-dab in the middle of the New Heartland. The goal is to raise money for the parks & wildlife department to help maintain existing resources, as well as fund their campaign to appeal to new anglers.

CASE STUDY

Festival organizers know this area well—because they're from here! Local brands and representatives also have personal insight on messaging that will appeal to these New Heartlanders. Still, a lot of research goes into making this event a success each year, from choosing the right music acts to deciding which vendors will have the most to offer festival goers. Their marketing and communications agency, Octagon, are New Heartlanders as well. So they were able to create a marketing strategy that spoke perfectly to area residents, resulting in big attendance numbers.

Two important core values are in play here. The event is designed in a way that's fun for the whole family. It's also a big win for the community, with attendees and local vendors coming together to raise money that will stay local.

The Toyota Texas Bass Classic uses almost all of the Five Channels of Access to pull off their legendary event.

Music: Festival organizers employ top country music acts each year. They know what their attendees want and give it to them in the form of big-name acts.

Food: Good BBQ is a sure win in the New Heartland. Not only will you find it here in abundance, but you'll sample the best of the best as a BBQ cook-off competition ensures every smoked meat lover goes home happy.

Outdoor: The whole festival is built around the three-day fishing tournament that is televised not only locally, but also nationally on NBC Sports.

Digital: The marketing team does a great job of using its social media channels and blog to promote the festival in the months and days leading up to the big event.

④

IMPLEMENT

(EXECUTION)

With this perfect culmination of New Heartland favorites in music, food, and outdoor activities, this Bass Classic keeps families coming back each year. Country music acts such as The Band Perry, Lee Brice, the Eli Young Band, Dierks Bentley, Gary Allan, Little Big Town, and Justin Moore play to huge crowds each night after the weigh-in. A BBQ cook-off sees dozens of teams competing for the best brisket, chicken, and ribs—to the delight of hungry attendees. And fishermen get to watch their favorite anglers compete for the big title, while hopefully picking up some tips along the way. A fantastic digital campaign helps with promotional efforts while keeping followers updated on the events as they occur.

The Toyota Texas Bass Classic is also a place where brands are able to connect with consumers in a fun and meaningful way. The title sponsor, Toyota, really does a great job activating their sponsorship by offering attendees the chance to try out their trucks on an off-road track that winds through mud pits and large mounds. Yamaha gets in on the action, as well, offering consumers the chance to test drive their ATV's through their challenging obstacle course. Bass Pro Shops gets the whole family involved with a Kids Zone, complete with a BB gun shooting range, kayak pool, and mechanical bull.

5

MEASURE
(EVALUATION & MEASUREMENT)

The Festival has become a staple of the area. More than sixty thousand people turn out every year. Last year, the festival raised $1.75 million for the Texas Parks & Wildlife Department!

For the 1.85 million anglers in Texas, this is great news. It's also a big deal for participating brands. Not only do they receive exposure on the local level, but this world-famous tournament is televised on NBC Sports. The Toyota Texas Bass Classic is a solid example of an integrated approach to winning over or just reinforcing a brand's positioning with the New Heartland consumer.

» Overlay New Heartland insights and language as you walk through the Five Step Process for Marketing to the New Heartland: Understand, Plan, Create, Implement, and Measure.

» Get to know the New Heartland audience—do your research so you understand current brand perceptions, both positive and negative.

» Remember you don't need to change your brand message, just the way it's delivered taking into account Core Values of Faith, Community, and Family as you create your campaign messaging and delivery.

» Remember to execute a plan that lets you build relationships and meet consumers where they are through key lifestyle channels such as Music, Food, Sports, Outdoors, and Social Media.

» Study and learn from other brands that engage well and have strong loyalty within the New Heartland.

SUMMARY

So how did you do? Is your creative resonating with the core values of the New Heartland? Does your campaign Speak American? Does it reach the New Heartlander in an authentic way in the places that are near and dear to them? Do you have checkpoints for your campaign to analyze and course correct?

I'd love to hear about your branding experiences as you work to build relationships with the New Heartland consumer. Connect at www.newheartlandgroup.com and we'll keep fine-tuning the best practices to help you build a sustainable brand in America's most-powerful cultural segment.

Consider yourself part of the Speak American brand team!

About the Author

Paul Jankowski is founder and chief brand strategist at Nashville-based New Heartland Group, and is a recognized thought leader on branding in the New Heartland. For more than two decades, he has helped some of the nation's leading brands including Pepsi, Pizza Hut, Lipton and Mountain Dew connect with the 60% of U.S. consumers in the New Heartland. In addition to his published works, Paul is a Forbes contributor on marketing to the New Heartland consumer, and keynote speaker on brand building, creating culturally-relevant messaging, and branded entertainment marketing.

Paul has served as chief marketing officer for Elvis Presley Enterprises, and held senior marketing positions with SFX Entertainment (Live Nation), Gibson Guitar Corp., and MCA Records. He has worked directly with many entertainers and professional athletes including Beyonce, Taylor Swift, Blake Shelton, Jason Aldean, Evander Holyfield and Elton John.

Co-founder of the TJ Martell Foundation's Nashville division, the music industry supported foundation that funds medical research for leukemia, cancer and AIDS, Paul received the Foundation's "From the Heart" award. He received his B.S. degree in Communications/Advertising from the University of Tennessee/Knoxville. He lives with his wife of 25 years and four children outside of Nashville.

About New Heartland Group

Founded in 2002 by brand strategist Paul Jankowski, New Heartland Group is the industry leader in helping brands connect with the 60% of U.S. consumers living in the New Heartland. Located in the Midwest, Southwest and most of the Southeast, the New Heartland is a powerful cultural segment that is largely misunderstood and underserved by advertisers. This massive group is connected to each other by a shared set of core values which guide key purchasing decisions.

Strategically located in Nashville, Tennessee, New Heartland Group helps clients stay relevant with the New Heartland consumer through ongoing research and cultural immersion. The agency offers a full portfolio of services focusing on brand strategy, content creation, digital marketing, branded entertainment and insights — all designed to help brands Speak American(tm). New Heartland Group has helped leading brands such as Pepsi, Pizza Hut, Lipton Iced Tea, Mountain Dew, B.B. King's Blues Clubs, and Stages West to understand and engage this crucial consumer segment.

Visit www.newheartlandgroup.com for more information.

ILLUSTRATION RESOURCES

1. "New Heartland Consumer Insights Study." June 2014. Conducted by Prince Market Research for New Heartland Group.

2. "Valero Energy Fortune 500 2014." Fortune. 2014. <http://fortune.com/fortune500/valero-energy-corporation-10/>

3. Kotkin, Joel. "The Cities Winning The Battle For Information Jobs 2014." Forbes. May 2014. <http://www.forbes.com/sites/joelkotkin/2014/05/27/the-cities-winning-the-battle-for-information-jobs-2014/>

4. Dann, Carrie. "Losing Faith: 21 Percent Say Religion 'Not That Important.'" NBC News. March 12, 2014. <http://www.nbcnews.com/politics/politics-news/losing-faith-21-percent-say-religion-not-important-n51256>

   "Religion | Gallup Historical Trends" GALLUP Poll. 2009. <http://www.gallup.com/poll/1690/religion.aspx>

   Newport, Frank. "Mississippi Most Religious State, Vermont Least Religious." GALLUP Well-Being. February 3, 2014. <http://www.gallup.com/poll/167267/mississippi-religious-vermont-least-religious-state.aspx>

   "New Heartland Consumer Insights Study." June 2014. Conducted by Prince Market Research for New Heartland Group.

5. "Religion | Gallup Historical Trends" GALLUP Poll. 2009. <http://www.gallup.com/poll/1690/religion.aspx>

6. Newport, Frank. "Mississippi Most Religious State, Vermont Least Religious." GALLUP Well-Being. February 3, 2014. <http://www.gallup.com/poll/167267/mississippi-religious-vermont-least-religious-state.aspx>

7. "National Brands Go Local via Social", Marketing News, April 2014.

8. "National Brands Go Local via Social", Marketing News, April 2014.

9. "United States of Smiles - The Search for the Happiest City in America." JetPac City Guides. December 4, 2013. <http://www.jetpac.com/blog/post/69033145344/united-state-of-smiles-the-search-for-the-happiest>

10. "New Heartland Consumer Insights Study." June 2014. Conducted by Prince Market Research for New Heartland Group.

Wasserman, Todd. "Report: 70% of Consumers Trust Brand Recommendations From Friends." Mashable. March 21, 2013. <http://mashable.com/2013/03/21/70-percent-brand-recommendations-friends/>

Consoli, John. "Nickelodeon Study Affirms Kids' Strong Influence on Family Purchasing Decisions." Broadcasting & Cable. August 22, 2012. <http://www.broadcastingcable.com/news/news-articles/nickelodeon-study-affirms-kids-strong-influence-family-purchasing-decisions/113500>

11. Davies, Alex and Nudelman, Mike. "Best-Selling Car In Every State [MAP]." Business Insider. November 20, 2013. <http://www.businessinsider.com/best-selling-car-in-every-state-map-2013-11>

12. Livingston, Gretchen and Parker, Kim. "Since the Start of the Great Recession, More Children Raised by Grandparents." PewResearch Social & Demographic Trends. September 9, 2010. <http://www.pewsocialtrends.org/2010/09/09/since-the-start-of-the-great-recession-more-children-raised-by-grandparents/>

Cohn, D'Vera; Livingston, Gretchen; Passel, Jeffrey S. and Wang, Wendy . "Barely Half of U.S. Adults Are Married – A Record Low." PewResearch Social & Demographic Trends. December 14, 2011. <http://www.pewsocialtrends.org/2011/12/14/barely-half-of-u-s-adults-are-married-a-record-low/>

El Nasser, Haya. "More People Claim Black-White Heritage." USAToday.com. September 30, 2011. <http://www.usatoday.com/news/nation/story/2011-09-29/black-white-race/50610998/1>

13. Birkner, Christine. "Crossing Borders." American Marketing Association. April 2014. <https://www.ama.org/publications/MarketingNews/Pages/crossing-borders.aspx>

"Connect with Country" CMA World Report. 2013. <http://www.cmaworld.com/cmaaddons/world/2013-ConnectwithCountry.pdf>

14. Birkner, Christine. "Crossing Borders." American Marketing Association. April 2014. <https://www.ama.org/publications/MarketingNews/Pages/crossing-borders.aspx>

"Connect with Country" CMA World Report. 2013. <http://www.cmaworld.com/cmaaddons/world/2013-ConnectwithCountry.pdf>

15. AmericanIdol.com

16. "New Heartland Consumer Insights Study." June 2014. Conducted by Prince Market Research for New Heartland Group.

17. "New Heartland Consumer Insights Study." June 2014. Conducted by Prince Market Research for New Heartland Group.

18. Tierney, Jim. "NASCAR Creates Brand Loyalty Through Unique Engagement for its Sponsors." Loyalty360. August 1, 2013. <http://loyalty360.org/resources/article/nascar-creates-brand-loyalty-through-unique-engagement-for-its-sponsors>

    "About NASCAR." NASCAR.com. December 20, 2013. <http://www.nascar.com/en_us/news-media/articles/about-nascar.html>

    "NASCAR Racing Statistics." Statistic Brain. January 14, 2014 <http://www.statisticbrain.com/nascar-racing-statistics/>

    "The Sports Facilities Advisory Deems Youth Sports and Sports-Related Travel 'Recession Resistant' – Youth Sporting Events Create $7 Billion in Economic Impact." PRWeb. November 25, 2013. <http://www.prweb.com/releases/2013/11/prweb11362596.htm>

    "College vs. Pro." Learfield Sports Report. 2012. <http://sportsaffiliates.learfield-sports.com/files/2012/11/College-vs.-Pro.pdf>

19. "New Heartland Consumer Insights Study." June 2014. Conducted by Prince Market Research for New Heartland Group.

20. Gaines, Cork. "The 25 Schools That Make The Most Money In College Football." Business Insider. January 16, 2013. <http://www.businessinsider.com/the-25-schools-that-make-the-most-money-in-college-football-2013-1?op=1>

21. "Texas Tops the List of the Best High School Football States in the Country." MaxPreps. October 3, 2013. <http://www.maxpreps.com/news/6trP5t2zy-0WYPX1S2zE7EQ/texas-tops-the-list-of-the-best-high-school-football-states-in-the-country.htm>

22. "National Survey of Fishing, Hunting, and Wildlife-Associated Recreation." U.S. Fish & Wildlife Service Report. 2011. <http://asafishing.org/uploads/ASA_fhw11-nat.pdf>

    "Wildlife and Sport Fish Restoration Program." U.S. Fish & Wildlife Service Report. 2011. <http://wsfrprograms.fws.gov/Subpages/NationalSurvey/2011_Survey.htm>

    "New Heartland Consumer Insights Study." June 2014. Conducted by Prince Market Research for New Heartland Group.

    "National Survey of Fishing, Hunting, and Wildlife-Associated Recreation." U.S. Fish & Wildlife Service Report. 2011. <https://www.census.gov/prod/2012pubs/fhw11-nat.pdf>

    Wade, Tyler. "Anglers spend $16 Billion A Year on Fishing." Bassmaster. November 19, 2012. <http://www.bassmaster.com/news/anglers-spend-16-billion-year-fishing>

    "Sportfishing in America: An Economic Force for Conservation." American Sportfishing Association. January 2013. <http://asafishing.org/uploads/2011_ASASportfishing_in_America_Report_January_2013.pdf>

"Number of Golf Courses in States — Tee Time." AARP. August 4, 2011. <http://www.aarp.org/entertainment/arts-leisure/info-08-2011/golf-courses.html>

23. "Sportfishing in America: An Economic Force for Conservation." American Sportfishing Association. January 2013. <http://asafishing.org/uploads/2011_ASASportfishing_in_America_Report_January_2013.pdf>

24. Adler, Emily. "The Race Among Social Networks for Engagement and Time-Spend Has Created New Winners and Losers." Business Insider. January 23, 2014. <http://www.businessinsider.com/social-media-engagement-statistics-2-2014-1>

Suresh, Shruti. "Social Media Statistics to Drive Engagement in 2014." Beta21. 2013. <http://beta21.circussocial.com/case-studies/social-media-statistics-to-drive-engagement-for-2014/>

"Facebook Statistics." Statistic Brain. July 1, 2014. <http://www.statisticbrain.com/facebook-statistics/>

"About." Twitter. 2014. <https://about.twitter.com/company>

Polard, Gillian. "5 Pinterest Stats to Consider." Social Media Today. October 20, 2013. <http://www.socialmediatoday.com/content/5-pinterest-stats-consider>

"20 Captivating Marketing Statistics [Infographic]." WebDAM. 2014. <http://info.webdam.com/2014-Marketing-Statistics-Infographic.html?aliId=1932138>

Sass, Erik. "Social Ad Spend To Pass $11 Billion By 2017." MediaPost. August 6, 2014. <http://www.mediapost.com/publications/article/231564/social-ad-spend-to-pass-11-billion-by-2017.html?edition=75095.>

25. "Mobile Continues to Steal Share of US Adults' Daily Time Spent with Media." eMarketer.com. April 22, 2014. <http://www.emarketer.com/Article/Mobile-Continues-Steal-Share-of-US-Adults-Daily-Time-Spent-with-Media/1010782>

26. New Heartland Group, 2014

27. "The New Multi-screen World: Understanding Cross-platform Consumer Behavior." Google Report. August 2012. <http://services.google.com/fh/files/misc/multiscreenworld_final.pdf>

28. Siwicki, Bill. "It's Official: Mobile Devices Surpass PCs in Online Retail." Internet Retailer. October 1, 2013.

29. New Heartland Group, 2014

REFERENCES

1. "New Heartland Consumer Insights Study." June 2014. Conducted by Prince Market Research for New Heartland Group.

2. "Latinas Are a Driving Force Behind Hispanic Purchasing Power in the US." *Nielsen Report*, August 2014.

3. "New Heartland Consumer Insights Study." June 2014. Conducted by Prince Market Research for New Heartland Group.

4. "Farms, Land in Farms, and Livestock Operations 2012 Summary." *USDA*, February 2013.

5. "Valero Energy Fortune 500 2014." *Fortune*, 2014.

6. Kotkin, Joel. "The Cities Winning The Battle For Information Jobs 2014." *Forbes*, May 2014.

7. "Taylor Swift Leads Billboard's 2014 Money Makers." *Billboard*, March 10, 2014.

8. Cassidy, Christina A. "Georgia's Film Industry Grows With 'Hunger Games' And 'Walking Dead.'" *Huffington Post*, April 28, 2013.

9. "Creating Jobs." *Motion Picture Association of America*, 2014.

10. "Medient to Build America's Largest Movie Studio in Effingham, Georgia." *Yahoo! Finance*, March 20, 2013.

11. "Adult Obesity—Centers for Disease Control and Prevention." 2011. 21 Aug. 2014 <http://www.cdc.gov/obesity/data/adult.html>

12. "Declining Childhood Obesity Rates—Where Are We Seeing the Most Progress?" Robert Wood Johnson Foundation—Health Policy Snapshot Report, September 2012.

13. Dann, Carrie. "Losing Faith: 21 Percent Say Religion 'Not That Important.'" NBC News, March 12, 2014.

14. "Religion | Gallup Historical Trends" Gallup Poll, 2009.

15. Newport, Frank. "Mississippi Most Religious State, Vermont Least Religious." *Gallup Well-Being*, February 3, 2014.

16. "New Heartland Consumer Insights Study." June 2014. Conducted by Prince

Market Research for New Heartland Group.

17. Carter, Bill. "'The Bible,' a Hit on Cable, Will Have Its Sequel on NBC." *The New York Times*, July 1, 2013.

18. "National Brands Go Local via Social," *Marketing News*, April 2014.

19. "United States of Smiles - The Search for the Happiest City in America." *JetPac City Guides*, December 4, 2013.

20. "Midwest Profile—Volunteering and Civic Life in the Midwest." *Corporation for National & Community Service*, 2009.

21. "Lifetime Mobility in the United States: 2010." *Census.gov*, November 2011.

22. "New Heartland Consumer Insights Study." June 2014. Conducted by Prince Market Research for New Heartland Group.

23. Cohn, D'Vera and Rich Morin. "Who Moves? Who Stays Put? Where's Home?" *PewResearch Social & Demographic Trends*, December 29, 2008.

24. Keller, Ed. "Word-of-Mouth Goes Mainstream, Is Now Measureable." *Advertising Age*, February 6, 2013.

25. "Social Networking Fact Sheet." *PewResearch Internet Project*, January 2014.

26. "New Heartland Consumer Insights Study." June 2014. Conducted by Prince Market Research for New Heartland Group.

27. Wasserman, Todd. "Report: 70% of Consumers Trust Brand Recommendations From Friends." *Mashable*, March 21, 2013.

28. Consoli, John. "Nickelodeon Study Affirms Kids' Strong Influence on Family Purchasing Decisions." *Broadcasting & Cable*. August 22, 2012.

29. Davies, Alex and Mike Nudelman. "Best-Selling Car In Every State [MAP]." *Business Insider*, November 20, 2013.

30. Livingston, Gretchen and Kim Parker. "Since the Start of the Great Recession, More Children Raised by Grandparents." *PewResearch Social & Demographic Trends*, September 9, 2010.

31. Cohn, D'Vera; Gretchen Livingston; Jeffrey S. Passel and Wendy Wang . "Barely Half of U.S. Adults Are Married—A Record Low." *PewResearch Social & Demographic Trends*, December 14, 2011.

32. El Nasser, Haya. "More People Claim Black-White Heritage." *USAToday.com*, September 30, 2011.

33. Birkner, Christine. "Crossing Borders." *American Marketing Association*, April 2014.

34. "Connect with Country" *CMA World Report*, 2013.

35. Ibid.

36. Birkner, Christine. "Crossing Borders." *American Marketing Association*. April 2014.

37. "CMA Awards Ratings Surge to Four-Year High." *CMA World*,November 7, 2013.

38. AmericanIdol.com

39. Sebastian, Michael. "Rolling Stone Planning New Website to Cover Country Music." *Advertising Age,* December 5, 2013.

40. Hampp, Andrew. "Pepsi Recruits Blake Shelton for 'Iconic Summer' Campaign, Preps Exclusive Giveaways for Beyonce Tour, MLB All-Star Game." *billboardbiz*, June 11, 2013.

41. "New Heartland Consumer Insights Study." June 2014. Conducted by Prince Market Research for New Heartland Group.

42. Kay, Alex. "Super Bowl Ad Costs: Latest Info on Cost of 2014 Super Bowl Commercials." *bleacher report*, February 2, 2014.

43. Callos, Alex. "Power Ranking All 124 College Football Stadiums." *bleacher report*, April 19, 2012.

44. "All-Division Attendance Mark Sets Records; Total Figure Tops 50 Million." *NCAA*, February 3, 2014.

45. "New Heartland Consumer Insights Study." June 2014. Conducted by Prince Market Research for New Heartland Group.

46. Gaines, Cork. "The 25 Schools That Make The Most Money In College Football." *Business Insider*, January 16, 2013.

47. "College vs. Pro." *Learfield Sports Report*, 2012.

48. "NASCAR Racing Statistics." *Statistic Brain*, January 14, 2014.

49. "About NASCAR." *NASCAR.com*, December 20, 2013.

50. Tierney, Jim. "NASCAR Creates Brand Loyalty Through Unique Engagement for its Sponsors." *Loyalty360*, August 1, 2013.

51. "About NASCAR." *NASCAR.com*, December 20, 2013.

52. "NASCAR Racing Statistics." *Statistic Brain*, January 14, 2014.

53. Scarborough. "NASCAR Fans Tune In for Daytona 500 & Plan on Purchasing New Wheels." *Nielsen Social*, February 22, 2013.

54. "Race Fans Continue to 'Embrace Engagement.'" *Sports Business Journal*, November 26, 2012.

55. "NASCAR Racing Statistics." *Statistic Brain*, January 14, 2014.

56. Brooks, Chad. "In Recession, Fortune 500 Turns to NASCAR." *Business News Daily*, August 15, 2012.

57. "Texas Tops the List of the Best High School Football States in the Country." *MaxPreps*, October 3, 2013.

58. "The Sports Facilities Advisory Deems Youth Sports and Sports-Related Travel 'Recession Resistant' — Youth Sporting Events Create $7 Billion in Economic Impact." *PRWeb*, November 25, 2013.

59. "National Survey of Fishing, Hunting, and Wildlife-Associated Recreation." *U.S. Fish & Wildlife Service Report*, 2011.

60. Ibid.

61. "Wildlife and Sport Fish Restoration Program." *U.S. Fish & Wildlife Service Report*, 2011.

62. "New Heartland Consumer Insights Study." June 2014. Conducted by Prince Market Research for New Heartland Group.

63. "National Survey of Fishing, Hunting, and Wildlife-Associated Recreation." *U.S. Fish & Wildlife Service Report*, 2011.

64. Wade, Tyler. "Anglers spend $16 Billion a Year on Fishing." *Bassmaster*, November 19, 2012.

65. "Sportfishing in America: An Economic Force for Conservation." *American Sportfishing Association*, January 2013.

66. "Number of Golf Courses in States—Tee Time." *AARP*, August 4, 2011.

67. Peterson, Tim. "Google Tests Way to Track Consumers from Mobile Browsers to the Apps They Use." *Ad Age*, August 7, 2014.

68. Lieb, Rebecca, and Jaimy Szymanski."Why Mobile Is Essential for Brand Marketing." *Altimeter Group*, August 13, 2014.

69. Tzeng, Emma. "Social Login: What CMOs Should Know – Infographic." *GIGYA Blog*, April 5, 2013.

70. "Mobile Continues to Steal Share of US Adults' Daily Time Spent with Media." *eMarketer.com*, April 22, 2014.

71. "New Heartland Consumer Insights Study." June 2014. Conducted by Prince Market Research for New Heartland Group.

72. Adler, Emily. "The Race Among Social Networks for Engagement and Time-Spend Has Created New Winners and Losers." *Business Insider*, January 23, 2014.

73. Suresh, Shruti. "Social Media Statistics to Drive Engagement in 2014." *Beta21*, 2013.

74. "Facebook Statistics." *Statistic Brain*, July 1, 2014.

75. Ibid.

76. "About." Twitter, 2014.

77. "Statistics." YouTube, 2013.

78. Polard, Gillian. "5 Pinterest Stats to Consider." *Social Media Today*, October 20, 2013.

79. "Share of Time Spent per Day with Major Media by US Adults, 2010-2013." eMarketer, 2013.

80. "20 Captivating Marketing Statistics [Infographic]." WebDAM, 2014.

81. Ibid.

82. "Retail Insight Center - Internet/Catalogue/TV." NRF Foundation, August 2014.

83. Sass, Erik. "Social Ad Spend to Pass $11 Billion by 2017." *MediaPost*, August 6, 2014.

84. "Global Trust in Advertising and Brand Messages." *Nielsen Reports and Insights*, April 10, 2012.

85. Suresh, Shruti. "Social Media Statistics to Drive Engagement in 2014." *Beta21*, 2013.

86. "About." Twitter, 2014.

87. Polard, Gillian. "5 Pinterest Stats to Consider." *Social Media Today*, October 20, 2013.

88. Hertzfeld, Esther. "Radisson Blu Gets More 'Social' with Guests." *Hotel Management*, August 5, 2014.

89. Berthiaume, Dan. "Survey: Seven-in-10 Consumers Say Digital Coupons Have Positive Impact." *Chain Store Age*, August 7, 2014.

90. "New Heartland Consumer Insights Study." June 2014. Conducted by Prince Market Research for New Heartland Group.

91. Ibid.

92. Chahal, Mindi. "Consistent Branding: Don't Mess With It." *Marketing Week*, May 30, 2013.

93. Ibid.

94. Olenski, Steve. "Using Branded Content in Your Content Marketing Arsenal." *Forbes*, March 25, 2013.

95. "Photo Release—Two Thirds of Brands, Agencies Say Branded Content Marketing Now Important to Their Marketing Mix." *The Wall Street Journal*, May 20, 2013.

96. "New Heartland Consumer Insights Study." June 2014. Conducted by Prince Market Research for New Heartland Group.

97. Colwyn, Susanne. "New Consumer Media Consumption Research." *Smart Insights*, March 13, 2014.

98. "New Heartland Consumer Insights Study." June 2014. Conducted by Prince Market Research for New Heartland Group.

99. Schultz, E.J. "Forecast: Sponsorship Spending Will Slow in 2014." *Ad Age*, January 7, 2014.

Notes

Notes

Notes

Notes

Notes